Endorsements for
The Urgency of the New Evangelization: Answering the Call, by Ralph Martin

"Christian faith is not a habit. It's not a useful moral code. It's not an exercise in nostalgia. It's a restlessness, a consuming fire in the heart to experience the love of Jesus Christ and then share it with others — or it's nothing at all. Ralph Martin compellingly captures in these pages the essence of the 'new evangelization' as a new Pentecost — and why conforming our lives to it is so vital for our own salvation and the salvation of the world around us."

— Most Reverend Charles J. Chaput, O.F.M. Cap.
Archbishop of Philadelphia

"In *The Urgency of the New Evangelization,* Ralph Martin provides the proper 'urgency' to the task of the New Evangelization. There is no urgency unless there is a call to holiness and evangelization founded on a personal grasp of the eternal consequences (heaven and hell) in this life of entering by the narrow gate (Mt 7:13). If we fail to grasp the presence of sin in our world and in our lives, there will be no need to be saved, and hence, no urgency.... This book is a must to set the course."

— Most Reverend Archbishop Joseph E. Kurtz
Archbishop of Louisville

"In *The Urgency of the New Evangelization: Answering the Call,* Ralph Martin proposes the clear rationale and compelling need for the whole Church to engage in a new evangelization. We have here a very accessible resource that I hope will help awaken and engage the laity in embracing the full implications of their Baptism and Confirmation."

— Most Reverend Paul S. Coakley, S.T.L.
Archbishop of Oklahoma City

"Be prepared! This text will challenge and unsettle you. With a prophetic passion and clarity, Ralph Martin reminds us of the reality of heaven and hell, entreating us urgently to seek for ourselves and to help lead others to 'the narrow gate … that leads to life' (Mt 7:13, 14)."

— Todd Graff, Director of Lay Formation,
Diocese of Winona

"Here is a book that surely lives up to its title. If this book does not create a sense of urgency to evangelize, nothing can. Ralph Martin masterfully develops a biblically based summons to the critical work of evangelizing, a work on which depends the very salvation of countless souls. I highly recommend this book as essential reading for every pastor, parent, catechist, leader — indeed, every member of the Church. It will light a passionate fire to evangelize in all who read it!"

— Msgr. Charles Pope, pastor, blogger,
and Our Sunday Visitor columnist

"Ralph Martin has been leading the charge for renewal in the Church for several decades. This new book draws upon his profound knowledge of what is necessary for the New Evangelization. He effectively establishes that the primary reason for the urgency of the New Evangelization is that the eternal destinies of people we love — indeed all people — are at stake. He also clearly delineates the way in which every Catholic can contribute toward its success."

"There is a lot of hype about the 'New Evangelization.' This book makes a clear, focused and biblical case for it, helpfully tracing the theme from the Second Vatican Council. After reading it, you are called to decision. That is rare. It is also most welcome. This is a work that combines theology with a zealous pastoral urgency. Read it."

"Ralph Martin's book raises the essential questions — Why mission? Why bother? — and explores them in ways that both challenge and comfort. By addressing the crisis of faith head-on, he reveals the necessary starting point for the New Evangelization. This book will provoke some powerful soul-searching. It is a valuable guide to a very necessary examination of conscience."

"'Like a voice crying out in the wilderness,' Ralph Martin accurately assesses the need for the New Evangelization exhorted by Pope John Paul II and encouraged by Pope Benedict XVI. A prophetic and practical call to what Christians must do to 'aid humanity in not falling' and to advance the full expression of the Good News of Jesus Christ 'for such a time as this.' Be prepared to be called into mission and ministry for the sake of the Kingdom of God!"

— Johnnette Benkovic, founder of
Women of Grace and EWTN host

"In *The Urgency of the New Evangelization*, Ralph Martin correctly identifies the need to evangelize and provides insights born of both faith and experience on how to do it. The book will be of particular value to the laity, many of whom continue to believe that the duty to evangelize falls mainly on the clergy and religious. Martin shows, from both Church documents and actual examples, the error of this view, and provides practical advice on how we laity can dispose ourselves to be instruments of building up of the Kingdom."

— Colin Donovan, S.T.L., Vice President
for Theology, EWTN

The Urgency

of the New Evangelization:

Answering the Call

The Urgency
of the New Evangelization:
Answering the Call

Ralph Martin

With a biblical perspective by
Mary Healy and Peter Williamson

Our Sunday Visitor Publishing Division
Our Sunday Visitor, Inc.
Huntington, Indiana 46750

Nihil Obstat:
Msgr. Michael Heintz, Ph.D.
Censor Librorum

Imprimatur:
✠ Kevin C. Rhoades
Bishop of Fort Wayne-South Bend
May 13, 2013

The Nihil Obstat and Imprimatur are official declarations that a book is free from doctrinal or moral error. It is not implied that those who have granted the Nihil Obstat and Imprimatur agree with the contents, opinions, or statements expressed.

Contents

Chapter I

What Is the New Evangelization?

Rooted in Vatican II

Pope John Paul II spoke about the need for a "new evangelization" multiple times during his pontificate. When he died, many wondered what would become of this emphasis. It soon became apparent that Pope Benedict XVI would not only continue the call for a "new evangelization" but make it an ongoing focus of the entire Church. Pope Benedict XVI "institutionalized" the major emphasis that Pope John Paul II put on the need for a "new evangelization" by establishing a Pontifical Council for the Promotion of the New Evangelization and choosing New Evangelization as the theme of the October 2012 World Synod of Bishops. Pope Francis in his first remarks after being elected Pope spoke of the responsibility to evangelize Rome. In continuing exhortations he has made clear that he is calling us all as individuals and as parochial communities to "get out of ourselves" and reach out to those who are not presently close to the Church. The roots though of the continuing papal emphasis on a "new evangelization" are located in the rationale and documents of Vatican II, the fiftieth anniversary of which we have recently commemorated. The Council was called out of a sense that an authentic renewal of the Church's life was necessary in order to more effectively communicate to the modern world the saving message of Christ.

As Cardinal Avery Dulles has pointed out, there was a significant shift in emphasis from Vatican I to Vatican II:

> A simple word count indicates the profound shift in focus. Vatican I, which met from 1869–1870, used the term gospel (*evangelium*) only once and never used the terms evangelize and evangelization. Less than a century later, Vatican II mentioned the gospel 157 times and used the verb evangelize eighteen times and the noun evangelization thirty-one times. When it spoke of evangelization, Vatican II generally meant the proclamation of the basic Christian message of salvation through Jesus Christ.[1]

Initial Confusion

For the first decade after Vatican II, though, the main focus of many seemed to be on issues such as the sharing of power within the Church, the setting up of consultative bodies such as parish and diocesan councils, the implementation of a vernacular liturgy, the turn toward Christian unity, dialogue with non-Christian religions, and dialogue with the modern world. At the same time there were multiple theological challenges directed to the teaching of the Church in the areas of sexual morality, the priesthood, and the very uniqueness and identity of Christ, which spread widespread confusion about what the Church still believed and taught. Some famous theologians gave lectures all over the world talking about Vatican II as "just the beginning" and pushing for more and more radical change, which led to a disregard for the amazingly beautiful and relevant documents themselves.

It wasn't until 1975 and the publication of Pope Paul VI's *Evangelii Nuntiandi* ("On Evangelization in the Modern World," henceforth abbreviated as EN) that some of the most foundational themes of Vatican II resurfaced. Both Pope Paul VI and Pope John Paul II often summarized the deepest purpose of the Council as renewal for the sake of evangelization. As Pope Paul VI stated it, the purposes of the Council "are definitively summed up in this single one: to make the Church of the twentieth century ever better fitted for proclaiming the gospel to the people of the twentieth century" (EN, 2). The popes have identified renewal in holiness as the primary renewal that the Council called for, and the primary outward fruit of such holiness, a "new evangelization."

As Pope John Paul II stated in his 1990 encyclical on evangelization, *Redemptoris missio* ("Mission of the Redeemer," henceforth abbreviated as RM):

> The call to mission derives, of its nature, from the call to holiness.... *The universal call to holiness* is closely linked to the *universal call to mission*. Every member of the faithful is called to holiness and to mission. (RM, 90)

What Is the New Evangelization?

Starting in 1983 Pope John Paul II began to frequently call for a "new evangelization." He made it clear that he wasn't calling for a new gospel, but a new effort, characterized by new "ardor, methods, and expression,"[2] and directed in a new way, not only to those who have never heard the gospel before, the traditional "mission territories," but now also to the lukewarm and de-Christianized traditionally Christian Western nations.

> The New Evangelization does not consist of a "new gospel."... Neither does it involve removing from the Gospel whatever seems difficult for the modern mentality to accept.... The New Evangelization has as its point of departure the certitude that in Christ there are "inexhaustible riches" (Eph 3:8) which no culture nor era can exhaust....

These riches are, first of all, Christ himself, his person, because he himself is our salvation.[3]

He distinguished "primary evangelization" directed toward those who have never heard the gospel before, "pastoral care" directed toward those who were living as believers but also perhaps needing a deeper conversion, and "new evangelization or re-evangelization" directed toward those from traditionally Christian cultures or backgrounds "where entire groups of the baptized have lost a living sense of the faith, or even no longer consider themselves members of the Church, and live a life far removed from Christ and his Gospel" (RM, 33). To state it in a simple way, what's primarily new about the "new evangelization" is whom it is directed toward, the baptized who are not living in an active relationship of discipleship with Jesus. It is also "new" in the passion and enthusiasm that Pope John Paul II has stated is essential for its success, along with an openness to the Holy Spirit to show us new methods and expressions of the faith that can communicate with people today.

The Urgency of a New Evangelization

As Pope John Paul II published his "vision or mission statement" for the Catholic Church as it entered the new millennium, *Novo Millennio Ineunte* ("At the Beginning of a New Millennium," henceforth abbreviated as NMI), he cited the collapse of Christian society as a primary reason for the need for a new evangelization and highlighted the role of the Holy Spirit in making the New Evangelization effective:[4]

> To nourish ourselves with the word in order to be "servants of the Word" in the work of evangelization: this is surely a priority for the Church at the dawn of the new millennium. Even in countries evangelized many centuries ago, the reality of a "Christian society" which, amid

all the frailties which have always marked human life, measured itself explicitly on Gospel values, is now gone. Today we must courageously face a situation which is becoming increasingly diversified and demanding, in the context of "globalization" and of the consequent new and uncertain mingling of peoples and cultures. Over the years, I have often repeated the summons to the New Evangelization. I do so again now, especially in order to insist that we must rekindle in ourselves the impetus of the beginnings and allow ourselves to be filled with the ardor of the apostolic preaching which followed Pentecost. We must revive in ourselves the burning conviction of Paul, who cried out: "Woe to me if I do not preach the Gospel" (1 Cor 9:16).

> This passion will not fail to stir in the Church a new sense of mission, which cannot be left to a group of "specialists" but must involve the responsibility of all the members of the People of God. Those who have come into genuine contact with Christ cannot keep him for themselves, they must proclaim him. A new apostolic outreach is needed, which will be lived as the everyday commitment of Christian communities and groups. (NMI, 40)

The collapse of Christian society is being experienced in the Catholic Church as a "wake-up call" to the need for a renewal of fervor, both for holiness and for evangelization, rooted in the continuing reality of Pentecost.

> Whole countries and nations where religion and the Christian life were formerly flourishing … are now put to a hard test…. Certainly the command of Jesus: "Go and preach the Gospel" always maintains its vital value and its ever-pressing obligation. Nevertheless, the *present situation* not only of the world but also of many parts of the Church, *absolutely demands that the word of Christ*

receive a more ready and generous obedience. Every disciple is personally called by name: no disciple can withhold making a response: "Woe to me if I do not preach the gospel" (1 Cor 9:16). (*Christifidelis laicis,* "Christ's Lay Faithful," henceforth abbreviated as CL, 33–34)

It is sobering to see the radical decline in the practice of the faith in traditionally strong Catholic areas of North America, not to mention what's happening in Europe and Oceania. The statistics from just one midwestern diocese are typical of what is happening in dozens and dozens of dioceses in New England, the Middle Atlantic States, the Midwest and Upper Midwest and in many other dioceses throughout the United States and Canada.

The statistics reported below track this drop in a large Midwestern diocese, but statistics that I've seen from other dioceses are very similar and are typical of the Catholic heartland.[5]

Last Ten Years

	2000	2010	
Infant Baptisms	16,294	9,544	42.4% decrease
Adult Baptisms	1,442	704	51.2% decrease
Full Communion with the Church	1,713	960	43.6% decrease
Catholic Marriages	3,641	1,649	45.3% decrease
Interfaith Marriages	1,657	783	52.7% decrease
Funerals	10,461	9,496	9.2% decrease
Parishes	313	273	12.8% decrease

The collapse of Christian culture, as weak and ambiguous as it was in some ways, has profoundly affected the beliefs and actions of baptized Catholics. Whether it be the decline in Mass attendance, the radical drop in vocations, the widespread breakup of Catholic marriages, the increasing frequency of cohabitation by Catholics before or instead of marriage, and the shrinking of family size, the statistics are widely known but nevertheless quite shocking.[6]

What these statistics indicate, among other things, is that there is something like an institutional collapse going on, evidenced by the vast numbers of schools closing; parishes merging, clustering, and closing; and the multiple assignments that many young priests now are asked to manage. Besides the institutional collapse there is evidence of a widespread repudiation of the teaching of Christ and the Church by vast numbers of Catholics. Even those who attend Mass regularly often embody a set of beliefs that are closer to the secular elites than the teaching of Christ. Despite many positive signs, the trends are not encouraging. The radical collapse of the Church in some of the traditionally most Catholic parts of the country is masked by the large Hispanic immigration that has kept the statistics reported on the total Catholic population relatively stable. But the same secularizing forces are at work among the traditionally Catholic immigrants, and the lack of sufficient numbers of Spanish-speaking priests doesn't bode well for the future.[7] The challenge of evangelical and Pentecostal churches that embody more values of the Hispanic culture than the typical Catholic Anglo parish does is also a significant factor.[8]

The fact that this radical drop in the statistics from the diocese given above has occurred in only a space of ten years is particularly disturbing. There seems to be a definite acceleration in the falling away from the Church. Another aspect of the crisis is the apparent lack of sacramental fruitfulness in the lives of many who still partake of the sacraments. One of the most dramatic indicators of this is the experience of many parishes when it comes to the Sacrament of Confirmation. As I've spoken to youth ministers, religious education directors, and pastors in many parts of North America, and in my classroom at the seminary, the most common difficulty that I've heard expressed when discussion turns to Confirmation is that the majority of youth confirmed are seldom seen in church again. The sacrament that is supposed to express and effect deeper, conscious commitment to being witnesses to the faith seems in many cases to result in directly the opposite. For many youth and their parents Confirmation seems to be a "ritual" that completes the list of what "good Catholics" are supposed to do, and therefore no further religious education or even Church attendance seems necessary. This virtually unanimous anecdotal evidence is verified in the various studies that have been done on where "youth" are at today.

One of the most cited of the contemporary youth researchers is Christian Smith and his team, who in a comprehensive survey of American youth pointed out that Catholic youth are in some ways in the greatest difficulty among all religiously affiliated youth as regards orthodox belief.

For example, 57% of teenage Catholics stated that they possibly or definitely believed in reincarnation. The authors conclude that even though the "shell" or "form" of traditional religion is there, it has been colonized by an alien spirit that they describe as "Moralistic Therapeutic Deism."[9]

Of course it would not be accurate to leave the impression that the "secular culture" is to blame for all of this. Years of silence about those aspects of the gospel that the contemporary culture is hostile to — the truths about sin, about heaven and hell, about the need for repentance, about the real meaning of discipleship, about the supreme value of knowing Christ — have contributed to the metamorphosis of Catholicism in the minds of many into a comforting religious ritual of indeterminate meaning. When the American bishops a few years ago commissioned an evaluation of catechetical text books in use over the previous twenty-five years they found a vast majority of them were "defective" in presenting one or more key doctrines of the Church, despite having *imprimaturs* or official approval by bishops for use in their dioceses.

When the eternal consequences that flow from what we choose to believe and how we choose to act are not spoken of for long periods of time, the silence on these dimensions of the Gospel is often taken to mean that they are no longer important, true, or relevant.

As one Australian commentator has pointed out, when the eternal consequences of believing and obeying or not believing and obeying are left fuzzy, "the essential faith of Catholics will then amount to no more than a vague theism with little specific moral content; just what it is for a large proportion of Catholics today."[10]

The collapse of doctrinal clarity is certainly a major contributor to the general indifference to the call to evangelization that has so insistently come from the Magisterium since Vatican II. Cardinal Ratzinger called it a "catastrophic collapse" of catechetics.

> The New Evangelization we need so urgently today is not to be attained with cleverly thought out ideas, however cunningly these are elaborated: the catastrophic failure of modern catechesis is all too obvious.[11]

Avery Dulles, in a foreword to a recent book on evangelization,[12] cites unsettling statistics:[13]

> Asked whether spreading the faith was a high priority of their parishes, 75 percent of conservative Protestant congregations and 57 percent of African American congregations responded affirmatively, whereas only 6 percent of Catholic parishes did the same. Asked whether they sponsored local evangelistic activities, 39 percent of conservative Protestant congregations and 16 percent of African American congregations responded positively as compared with only 3 percent of Catholic parishes. Converts to Catholicism often report that on their spiritual journey they received little or no encouragement from Catholic clergy whom they consulted.

All of this forms the backdrop for the increasingly urgent calls coming from the papacy to dedicate ourselves to a "new evangelization." As Pope John Paul II put it in his 1990 encyclical on evangelization:

I sense that the moment has come to commit all of the Church's energies to a new evangelization and to the mission *ad gentes*. No believer in Christ, no institution of the Church can avoid this supreme duty: to proclaim Christ to all peoples. (RM, 3)

Cardinal Avery Dulles cited the great significance of this turn toward evangelization:

In my judgment the evangelical turn in the ecclesial vision of Popes Paul VI and John Paul II is one of the most surprising and important developments in the Catholic Church since Vatican II.... All of this constitutes a remarkable shift in the Catholic tradition.... Today we seem to be witnessing the birth of a new Catholicism that, without loss of its institutional, sacramental, and social dimensions, is authentically evangelical.... Catholic spirituality at its best has always promoted a deep personal relationship with Christ. In evangelizing we are required to raise our eyes to him and to transcend all ecclesiocentrism. The Church is of crucial importance but is not self-enclosed. It is a means of drawing the whole world into union with God through Jesus Christ.... Too many Catholics of our day seem never to have encountered Christ. They know a certain amount about him from the teaching of the Church, but they lack direct personal familiarity.... The first and highest priority is for the Church to proclaim the good news concerning Jesus Christ as a joyful message to all the world. Only if the Church is faithful to its evangelical mission can it hope to make its distinctive contribution in the social, political, and cultural spheres.[14]

Despite the sobering statistics, the call to a new evangelization will not be met with the passionate response the popes are calling for if we don't address the fundamental question: Why bother? Is the Church's self-preservation adequate motivation? For many people, it is not.

Chapter II

Why Bother?

Many reasons are given why it is important that there be a new evangelization. Chief among them seems to be the sober realization that traditionally Christian and Catholic countries are now under powerful assault by secularist and even anti-Christian forces. As a result many millions of our fellow believers may still have the name of Christian or Catholic but are no longer living as disciples of Christ or even understanding any more what it would mean to do so. This shows up not only in declining Church attendance but in the erosion of belief and morality even among those who still do attend.

Other reasons that are given to demonstrate the need for a new evangelization include theological reasons that show that evangelization is the primary mission of the Church, and that we have been explicitly commanded by Christ to evangelize. Mention is also frequently made about how becoming a Christian fulfills human nature, gives us eternal life and brings us to salvation, rescuing us from sin, with an occasional mention of Satan as well.

But even though these words are spoken and written, they often fail to "connect" with any sense of urgency because of a prevailing mentality that dulls our perception of the urgency for evangelization.

If I were to describe how very many of our fellow Catholics, as well as believers in the wider culture, look at these matters today, I would describe it like this: "Broad and wide is the way that leads to salvation/heaven and almost everybody is on that way. Narrow and difficult is the path that leads to condemnation/hell and very few, if any, are on that road." Sometimes it is acknowledged that particularly bad people like Hitler or Stalin may be in hell.

Now, the problem with this way of looking at things is that it is the exact opposite of what Jesus tells us about our situation in the Gospel.

> "Enter by the narrow gate; for the gate is wide and the way is easy, that leads to destruction, and those who enter by it are many. For the gate is narrow and the way is hard, that leads to life, and those who find it are few." (Mt 7:13–14)

Or, consider a parallel passage in Luke:

> And someone said to him, "Lord, will those who are saved be few?" And he said to them, "Strive to enter by the narrow door; for many, I tell you, will seek to enter and will not be able." (Lk 13:23–24)

Or consider the frequently repeated and unambiguous words of Jesus about the separation of humanity that will occur at the final judgment.

> "He who sows the good seed is the Son of man; the field is the world, and the good seed means the sons of the kingdom; the weeds are the sons of the evil one, and the enemy who sowed them is the devil; the harvest is the close of the age, and the reapers are angels. Just as the weeds are gathered and burned with fire, so will it be at the close of the age. The Son of man will send his angels, and they will gather out of his kingdom all causes of sin and all evildoers, and throw them into the furnace of fire, where there will be weeping and gnashing of teeth. Then the righteous will shine like the sun in the kingdom of their Father. He who has ears, let him hear." (Mt 13:37–43)

And from John's Gospel:

For God so loved the world that he gave his only begotten Son, that whoever believes in him should not perish, but have eternal life. God sent the Son into the world, not to condemn the world, but that the world might be saved through him. He who believes in him is not condemned, he who does not believe is condemned already, because he has not believed in the name of the only begotten Son of God. (Jn 3:16–18)

"Do not marvel at this; for the hour is coming when all who are in the tombs will hear his voice and come forth, those who have done good, to the resurrection of life, and those who have done evil, to the resurrection of judgment." (Jn 5:28–29)

Now Jesus didn't say these things because this is how things have to be; or because this is how he wants them to be; but simply because this is how things were when he looked out at the situation of the Jewish people in his time. And are our times any better?

Perhaps at certain high points of Christian culture "many" were on the way to salvation, and "fewer" on the way to condemnation, but in our time it is clear that the main river of culture is flowing ever more swiftly toward destruction.

We also know that Jesus was "broken hearted" about the prospect of so many being lost by their own choice when he wept as he foresaw their destruction on the hill overlooking Jerusalem (Lk 19:41). We also know that people who are presently on the wide path that leads to destruction could leave that path and set out on the narrow path that leads to life before they die and be saved. Of course, what evangelization is all about is inviting people to believe and repent and leave the wide path and set out on the narrow path that is so true, good, and blessed, the path that turns out to be Jesus himself.

But, some might ask, wasn't this picture of how things are changed by Vatican II? Aren't we to have a more positive outlook about most people being saved? Well, let's see exactly what Vatican II does teach about this most important of all issues.

One of the things that has led people to believe that a "broader" view of how many are saved has been taught by Vatican II is a text in the Constitution on the Church (*Lumen gentium*, "Light of the Nations," henceforth abbreviated as LG), 16.

This text clearly teaches that it is possible — under certain specific circumstances — for people to possibly be saved if they haven't heard the Gospel.

> Those who, through no fault of their own, do not know the Gospel of Christ or his Church, but who nevertheless seek God with a sincere heart, and moved by grace, try in their actions to do his will as they know it through the dictates of their conscience — those too may achieve eternal salvation....

What are the conditions? First, that their ignorance of the gospel is not their own fault. Secondly, that nevertheless, they are sincerely seeking God and desiring to know his will, and third, that they are living in conformity with the light and grace that God is giving them.

What kind of surrender to God is implied in these conditions? A footnote in the text refers to previous magisterial doctrinal clarifications that indicate that what grace moves people in this situation to is not just a vague belief in God but to a personal surrender to light and grace that God gives (supernatural faith) that leads to a conformity of one's life to the truth revealed (supernatural charity).[15]

When people hear that Vatican II taught that it is possible under certain very specific circumstances for people who have never heard the Gospel to be saved, they often go on to make a huge leap of logic — passing from a "possibility" to a presumed certainty, believing that for the most part people in this situation are saved. But this is a very defective understanding of the teaching of Vatican II. The last three sentences of this text are almost universally ignored even by well-known theologians who discuss this issue, and we must pay careful attention to them.

> But very often, deceived by the Evil One, men have become vain in their reasonings, have exchanged the truth of God for a lie and served the world rather than the Creator (cf. Rom 1:21, 25). Or else, living and dying in this world without God, they are exposed to ultimate despair. Hence to procure the glory of God and the salvation of all these, the Church, mindful of the Lord's command, "preach the Gospel to every creature" (Mk 16:16) takes zealous care to foster the missions. (LG, 16)

Even though it is theoretically possible for people who have never heard the Gospel to be saved, the actual situation in which all human beings find themselves is not "neutral." We are engulfed in the strong disordered desires of original sin, personal sin, an environment and culture that lead to sin, and the continuing work of the devil to deceive and destroy. If, as Paul teaches in Ephesians 6, we are the target of hostile spiritual powers who continually direct "fiery darts" toward us to affect our thinking, emotions, and actions, what is to become of those who are not aware of this spiritual warfare and don't have or utilize the "shield of faith" to extinguish these fiery darts? That is why the Council clearly teaches that "very often" the possibility of being saved without hearing the Gospel has not been actualized and people, for the sake of their salvation, need urgently to be called to faith, repentance, and baptism — the purpose of evangelization.

But not only are the eternal destinies of people who have never heard the Gospel in grave jeopardy but also the eternal destinies of Catholics who may have been baptized and may have some self-identification as Catholics but who are not living as disciples of Christ.

This is what Vatican II teaches about the situation of many Catholics:

> Even though incorporated into the Church, one who does not however persevere in charity is not saved. He remains indeed in the bosom of the Church, but "in body" not "in heart." All children of the Church should nevertheless remember that their exalted condition results, not from their own merits, but from the grace of Christ. If they fail to respond in thought, word and deed to that grace, not only shall they not be saved, but they shall be the more severely judged. (LG 14)

Not everyone who says "Lord, Lord" will be saved but only those who do the will of the Father (Mt 7:21–23). It is clearly not enough simply to be baptized, or even go to Church, to be saved: what is necessary is the faith that leads to obedience, to discipleship.

We are now in a position to give the most fundamental answer to the question we asked at the beginning of this chapter. Why bother to evangelize? Because the eternal destinies — heaven or hell — of many millions of our fellow Catholics, not to mention, many millions of countless others, are hanging in the balance. Christianity is not just an optional enrichment possibility for human life — but a message that truly is a matter of life or death, heaven or hell. If we truly love our family members, our neighbors, our fellow parishioners, or those who used to be our fellow parishioners, we're not only going to pray for them to find good jobs and get healed of physical illnesses but we're going to pray, suffer, love, and witness to the One who can save, for the sake of their salvation. We're going to say "yes" to the Popes' and the Spirit's call to participate in the "new evangelization."

Chapter III

Our Role in the New Evangelization

The Urgency of Lay Evangelization

The risen Christ has given leadership gifts to the Church: apostles, prophets, evangelists, teachers, and pastors, not to do the whole work of the Church but "to equip the saints for the work of ministry" (Eph. 4:12). The role of the priest, or laypeople employed by the Church, is not to carry out the mission of the Church all by themselves but to activate baptized Catholics into lives of holiness and mission.[16] There has been a long tendency in Catholicism for the laity to take a relatively passive role and expect the leaders to serve them. Sometimes leaders have fallen into this habit of relating as well. But as the Scripture indicates, and common sense reveals, there is no way that the mission of the Church can succeed without every baptized Catholic taking an active role. In addition, when one reflects upon what the job description of a Catholic pastor really is, as laid out in Canon Law, it becomes even more obvious that an active and involved laity is essential.

The Code of Canon Law makes clear that the pastor of the parish is responsible for all those who live within its boundaries, not just the "practicing Catholics."

> The Pastor … is to make every effort with the aid of the Christian faithful, to bring the gospel message also to those who have ceased practicing their religion or who do not profess the true faith. (Canon 528)

For many centuries the predominant understanding of Catholics in the "first world" was that evangelization was something that especially dedicated people (priests, nuns, and the occasional professional lay missionary), did in the "third world." But as both Pope John Paul II and Pope Benedict XVI have pointed out, the territory that an average Catholic parish covers in Europe or North America or Australia, for example, now may include people from different cultures and religions who have never heard the gospel before, as well as people who perhaps come from "Christian backgrounds" but no longer follow Christ, and an even smaller number of those who actually live as disciples. In other words, "primary evangelization," "new evangelization or re-evangelization" and "pastoral care" are all now part of the average Catholic pastor's job description although few have been rewritten to adequately express the new situation, nor has seminary training fully grasped the implications for the needed revision in preparation for ordination.[17]

While implementation of the New Evangelization on the parish level is just at its beginning stages, here and there priests and parishes have made the transition from "maintenance to mission" and developed a more evangelistic mentality as part of the fabric of Catholic parish life.[18]

Also, there has been a very widespread acceptance of the need for a new evangelization in leadership circles. Many bishops and bishops' conferences have affirmed the need for a new evangelization, and have issued pastoral letters[19] to that effect, faced as they are, with declining membership and the growth of a hostile culture in the Christian "heartlands." Given the general aging of the Catholic priesthood in the United States, Canada, Europe, and Oceania, along with greatly reduced numbers, there is generally little energy or time to reflect on the change of mentality that is needed to address the new situation of de-Christianization. Calls to a "new evangelization" are generally perceived by overworked clergy as a demand to add just another burden to their already overburdened responsibilities. It is generally seen as another burden, perhaps to be satisfied by appointing a committee, or in a few cases, hiring an "evangelist," or occasionally holding special evangelization events. A priest friend has decided in his parish not to have an evangelization "committee" but rather an evangelization "task force," which he hopes will move more quickly from discussion to action.

Clearly what Vatican II and the recent popes have been calling for is not satisfied by such steps, as useful as they may be. As Pope John Paul II put it in talking about the need to recover the fire of the early Church following Pentecost if the New Evangelization is to be effective:

> This passion will not fail to stir in the Church a new sense of mission, which cannot be left to a group of 'specialists' but must involve the responsibility of all the members of the People of God. Those who have come into genuine contact with Christ cannot keep him for themselves, they must proclaim him. A new apostolic outreach is needed, which will be lived as the everyday commitment of Christian communities and groups. (NMI, 40)

The message here is that the call to evangelization is addressed to each Christian and can't be delegated to "specialists" or committees. Obviously the role of the priest is absolutely crucial in teaching lay Catholics the reality of their call to holiness and evangelization, instructing them in their meaning, and guiding them in their mission. Nor is it adequate to occasionally have special evangelization events, as useful as they may be. What is being called for and what is necessary is evangelization becoming part of the baptized Catholic's fundamental identity and part of their everyday way of life.

There has been a tendency, however, in Post-Vatican II Catholicism to drift into an understanding of this call to lay mission that diverges significantly from what Vatican II actually says.[20] On the one hand, many interpret the call to apostolate as a call to "power sharing" and assign roles to laypeople within the Church that aren't really evangelistic. A lot of the focus has been, and continues to be, on laypeople becoming "active" within the church, i.e. doing readings at Mass, becoming "extraordinary" ministers of the Eucharist, joining parish councils, and serving on committees.

Recently some have attempted to correct this view by keeping the roles of priests and laity distinct. They point out that the specific nature of the lay apostolate is "secular" and should focus on the influence on culture and politics through promoting Christian values.

This emphasis on the secular quality of lay mission is usually silent about the responsibility to directly speak to people about Christ, with a view toward conversion.

The actual documents, however, could not be clearer, and more balanced on these points.

The *Decree on the Apostolate of Lay People* (henceforth abbreviated as DLA) identifies three fields of lay participation in the mission of the Church: 1) the mission of evangelization and sanctification; 2) the mission of renewing the temporal order; 3) the mission of mercy and charity. And while this document and others identify the layperson's unique presence in the secular order as irreplaceable, it goes on to make some remarkable statements about the priority of direct evangelization precisely in the secular environments that laypersons inhabit.

> The Church's mission is concerned with the salvation of men; and men win salvation through the grace of Christ and faith in him. The apostolate of the Church therefore, and of each of its members, aims primarily at announcing to the world by word and action the message of Christ and communicating to it the grace of Christ.... Laymen

have countless opportunities for exercising the apostolate of evangelization and sanctification. The very witness of a Christian life, and good works done in a supernatural spirit, are effective in drawing men to the faith and to God.... This witness of life, however, is not the sole element in the apostolate; the true apostle is on the lookout for occasions of announcing Christ by word, either to unbelievers to draw them towards the faith, or to the faithful to instruct them, strengthen them, and incite them to a more fervent life.... (DLA, 6)

The documents make clear that even if a layperson's primary field of mission is in the political, economic, or social sphere or in doing works of charity, he or she continues to have an obligation to directly proclaim Christ by word, with a view toward leading others to conversion or deeper faith.

This apostolate ... must not exclude any good, spiritual or temporal, that can be done for them. Genuine apostles are not content, however, with just this: they are earnest also about revealing Christ by word to those around them. It is a fact that many men cannot hear the Gospel and come to acknowledge Christ except through the laymen they associate with. (DLA, 13)

As Pope John Paul II put it,

The Council ... has written as never before on the nature, dignity, spirituality, mission and responsibility of the lay faithful. (CL, 2, 9)

The Council went beyond previous interpretations [of the lay faithful] which were predominantly negative. Instead it opened itself to a decidedly positive vision and displayed a basic intention of asserting *the full belonging of the lay faithful to the Church and to its mystery* ... sharers in the priestly, prophetic and kingly office of Christ. (CL, 9)

Taking Advantage of Opportunities to Share Our Faith

The call to include direct witnessing to Christ, in word as well as in the example of our lives, doesn't mean that we have to run out to the street corner with a sign around our neck calling for repentance. There are many "natural" ways of sharing the good news of the person of Jesus with others. For example, when there are events in our parish or diocese that include opportunities to hear a dynamic presentation of the Gospel, rather than just thinking about whether we will get anything out of it or not, we should always be thinking about who in our circle of contacts we could invite to go with us. We should consider who could really benefit by a relationship, or renewed relationship, with the Lord. Or, when we've listened to an inspiring or informative CD or read a good book on the faith, think about who in our circle of contacts might benefit from being asked to listen or read, and then asking for their feedback. Also, I've found that when I'm alert to opportunities to speak about my faith I notice a lot more opportunities than when I just drift along "minding my own business"!

Because of my involvement in the Cursillo Movement and Catholic Charismatic Renewal I have become used to sharing my "testimony" when opportunities to do so arise. What I've discovered, though, is that many people have never given much thought to how God has acted in their lives. Now at Sacred Heart Seminary in Detroit at the beginning of every class I have one of the students give his testimony. I direct him to share it without using jargon or "in" words so that an unbeliever or fallen away Catholic would be able to relate to it. I ask seminarians and priests not to tell how they discerned a calling to the priesthood but how they came to discover the reality of God in their lives. This is a struggle for some, but eventually almost everyone reaches the point where they can briefly give an account of how God became real in their lives in such a way that unbelievers could relate to it.

Also, sometimes when we've spent a weekend at a faith event, when people ask us what we've done during the weekend, rather than default to the sports event we watched after we got home, tell them the truth! Tell them about what you attended and what you "got out of it" to help you know the Lord better, and see where the conversation might lead.

Sometimes it's helpful to confront, in advance, the fears we have of being a witness. What are some of the negative responses we might get? Well, sometimes people may give us a cold stare and ignore what we've just said or change the topic. We can probably handle that, right? Remember all the rejection Jesus got but he kept on going, knowing only some of the seed he was sowing would sprout and bear fruit. We need to just keep on "sowing seeds" and recognize that some of the seed will be snatched away by the devil immediately, some will only have very shallow roots and wilt and die, and some will sprout up but over time be choked off by the cares and anxieties of life. But some will strike deep roots and bear much fruit. We also need to recognize that we will often be unable to really assess the effectiveness of our words but simply need to know that we've played a role, however small, in advancing the kingdom and giving people a chance to hear and be saved. Some plant, some water, and some see the growth.

Now, what's the worst possible thing that could happen to us in bearing witness to Christ? Well, someone may pull out a gun and kill us. As disturbing as that may initially sound, it's actually the best possible outcome: die as a martyr and go right to heaven! No more worries about credit card payments, doctors' appointments, diets, exercise, or relationship difficulties.

A Christian can't lose. For those who love God, he arranges that everything that he wills or permits, even the negative things, will work for our good. This should give us a great freedom and confidence as we embrace the call to evangelize.

And we should take heart that many are beginning to respond and we will not be alone. The "especially urgent invitation" that the Council has issued to the lay faithful is finding a response.

Often "repressed and buried" Christian powers are coming to life (CL 2, 23). "The commitment of the laity to the work of evangelization is changing ecclesial life…. Above all, there is a new awareness that missionary activity *is a matter for all Christians,* for all dioceses and parishes, Church institutions and associations" (RM, 2).

It is clear that for many who bear the name of Catholic a more "genuine contact with Christ" is needed for such a call to evangelization to even begin to make sense. Pope Paul VI makes clear that evangelization needs to start with the Church herself.

Even for those who are considered "devout" Catholics, a real conversion is needed, to seeing themselves not just as concerned with their own holiness and works of Christian service but consumed with a passion to share Christ with others.

May our "yes" to the call to holiness and to the call to evangelization, be ever deeper and may the life of Christ shine forth from our faces and the face of the Church so that as many as possible might be saved!

For this, of course, a "new Pentecost" is needed, appropriated on a personal level.

Chapter IV

A New Pentecost for the New Evangelization

The Papal Insistence on the Need for a "New Pentecost"

From the prayer of Pope John XXIII for the Council, asking God to send us a "new Pentecost," through Pope Benedict XVI's call for prayer for a renewal of Baptism and Confirmation, the "baptism in the Spirit," the popes have strongly emphasized the need the Church and each of us has to experience today the work of the Spirit as described in the Acts of the Apostles. As one surveys the persistent calls for a rediscovery or reappropriation of the work of the Holy Spirit as first experienced at Pentecost, one is struck by the fervor and depth of conviction in these repeated pleas. Sometimes even a note of desperation.[21]

Pope Paul VI

As Pope Paul VI put it in *Evangelii Nuntiandi*: "In our day, what has happened to that hidden energy of the Good News, which is able to have a powerful effect on man's conscience?" (4)[22]

He identifies a lack of fervor that "comes from within" and is "manifested in fatigue, disenchantment, compromise, lack of interest and above all lack of joy and hope" as a major obstacle to evangelization and exhorts us "always to nourish spiritual fervor" (80).

Pope Paul VI identifies the Holy Spirit as the source of spiritual ardor and points out the difference in the disciples before and after Pentecost. "It must be said that the Holy Spirit is the principal agent of evangelization: it is He who impels each individual to proclaim the Gospel, and it is He who in the depths of consciences causes the word of salvation to be accepted and understood. But it can equally be said that He is the goal of evangelization.…"

Pope Paul VI then talks about signs of the Spirit's action that he sees happening, calling the current time a "privileged moment of the Spirit."

> We live in the Church at a privileged moment of the Spirit. Everywhere people are trying to know Him better as the Scripture reveals Him. They are happy to place themselves under His inspiration. They are gathering about Him; they want to let themselves be led by Him.… It is not by chance that the great inauguration of evangelization took place on the morning of Pentecost, under the inspiration of the Spirit. (*Evangelii Nuntiandi* 75)

> The world is calling for evangelizers to speak to it of a God whom the evangelists themselves should know and be familiar with as if they could see the invisible. (*Evangelii Nuntiandi* 76)

> Was it not an inner renewal of this kind that the recent Council fundamentally desired? Assuredly we have here a work of the Spirit, a gift of Pentecost. One must also recognize a prophetic intuition on the part of our predecessor John XXIII, who envisaged a kind of new Pentecost as a fruit of the Council. We too have wished to place ourself in the same perspective and in the same attitude of expectation. Not that Pentecost has ever ceased to be an

actuality during the whole history of the Church, but so great are the needs and the perils of the present age, so vast the horizon of mankind drawn toward world coexistence and powerless to achieve it, that there is no salvation for it except in a new outpouring of the gift of God. (*Gaudete in Domino*) [23]

And:

> More than once we have asked ourselves what the greatest needs of the Church are … what is the primary and ultimate need of our beloved and holy Church? We must say it with holy fear because as you know, this concerns the mystery of the Church, her life: this need is the Spirit … the Church needs her eternal Pentecost; she needs fire in her heart, words on her lips, a glance that is prophetic.[24]

Pope John Paul II

Almost from the time he first mentioned the need for a "new evangelization" in Haiti in 1983 Pope John Paul II equally emphasized the need for a "new Pentecost." In *Christifideles laici* he interprets the whole post-conciliar spiritual renewal that has happened in the Catholic Church, characterized by renewal movements and the awakening of the laity to mission, as "a renewed outpouring of the Spirit of Pentecost" (2). Like Pope Paul VI before him, he devoted considerable attention in his encyclical *Redemptoris Missio* to the role of the Holy Spirit in energizing the mission of the Church. It was the "experience of Pentecost" that enabled the disciples to become "*witnesses* and *prophets*"(24).

Despite years of teaching and formation "they proved to be incapable of understanding his [Jesus'] words and reluctant to follow him along the path of suffering and humiliation. The Spirit transformed them into courageous witnesses to Christ and enlightened heralds of his word. It was the Spirit himself who guided them along the difficult and new paths of mission" (87).

Pope John Paul II's continued calls for a new Pentecost and a new evangelization and his steadfast welcome of renewal movements as a "hope for the Church" were based in part on an acute awareness of the depth of the challenges we face in preaching the gospel in the midst of an aggressive, international, pagan culture.

> We often experience the dramatic situation of the first Christian community, which witnessed unbelieving and hostile forces 'gathered together against the Lord and his Anointed' (Acts 4:26). Now as then, we must pray that God will grant us boldness in preaching the Gospel; we must ponder the mysterious ways of the Spirit and allow ourselves to be led by him into all the truth (cf. Jn 16:13). (87)

On the eve of the feast of Pentecost, in 1998, Pope John Paul II asked representatives of all the renewal movements of the Church to join with him to celebrate the outpouring of the Spirit. Over five hundred thousand people from more than fifty different movements came. In his address on this occasion he gathered together the teaching of Scripture and Vatican II on the reality of Pentecost and the gifts of the Spirit, and proclaimed it with urgency and passion, in the light of their actual embodiment in the various renewal movements and communities. He began:

> The Church's self-awareness (is) based on the certainty that Jesus Christ is alive, is working in the present and changes life.... With the Second Vatican Council, the Comforter recently gave the Church ... a renewed Pentecost, instilling a new and unforeseen dynamism.
>
> Whenever the Spirit intervenes, he leaves people astonished. He brings about events of amazing newness; he radically changes persons and history. This was the unforgettable experience of the Second Vatican Ecumenical Council during which, under the guidance of the same Spirit, the Church rediscovered the charismatic dimension as one of her constitutive elements: "It is not only through

the sacraments and the ministrations of the Church that the Holy Spirit makes holy the people, leads them and enriches them with his virtues. Allotting his gifts according as he wills (cf. 1 Cor 12:11), he also distributes special graces among the faithful of every rank ... makes them fit and ready to undertake various tasks and offices for the renewal and building up of the Church" (*Lumen gentium*, n. 12).

With these words Pope John Paul II boldly proclaimed the teaching of Vatican II, namely, that the charismatic workings of the Holy Spirit are an essential and complementary reality to the Spirit's working through the sacramental and hierarchical dimensions of the Church's existence. The pope also honestly acknowledged that the charismatic dimension, important as it is, was nevertheless in a way forgotten, or overshadowed by a perhaps too exclusive emphasis on the sacramental and hierarchical; and that it required a special action of the Holy Spirit in the Second Vatican Council to bring the Church back to an awareness of the importance of this "constitutive" dimension.

The pope also made this explicit: "The institutional and charismatic aspects are co-essential as it were to the Church's constitution. They contribute, although differently, to the life, renewal and sanctification of God's People. It is from this providential rediscovery of the Church's charismatic dimension that before and after the Council, a remarkable pattern of growth has been established for ecclesial movements and new communities.... You present here, are the tangible proof of this 'outpouring' of the Spirit."

The pope then made this extraordinary plea to all Christians: "Today, I would like to cry out to all of you gathered here in St. Peter's Square and to all Christians: Open yourselves docilely to the gifts of the Spirit! Accept gratefully and obediently the charisms which the Spirit never ceases to bestow on us!"[25]

As Pope John Paul II worked to prepare the Church for the challenges and opportunities of the third millennium, he published in 2001 *Novo Millennio Ineunte* in which he set out to "decipher" what the Holy Spirit had been saying to the Church from Vatican II until the beginning of the new millennium. This is a remarkable document that attempts to read the signs of the times and declare what the Pope believed the Spirit to be communicating to us at this moment of history. The document draws an explicit connection between the current historical situation of the Church, the main feature of which is the collapse of Christendom, and the need for a new evangelization. This in turn necessitates a rediscovery of the power of the Spirit as the first Christians experienced it on the day of Pentecost. We have already commented on certain aspects of this text earlier, but now we need to read it with attentiveness to its emphasis on the importance of Pentecost.

> Even in countries evangelized many centuries ago, the reality of a "Christian society" which, amid all the frailties which have always marked human life, measured itself explicitly on Gospel values, is now gone. Today we must courageously face a situation which is becoming increasingly diversified and demanding, in the context of "globalization" and of the consequent new and uncertain mingling of peoples and cultures. Over the years, I have often repeated the summons to the New Evangelization. I do so again now, especially in order to insist that we must rekindle in ourselves the impetus of the beginnings and allow ourselves to be filled with the ardor of the apostolic preaching which followed Pentecost. We must revive in ourselves the burning conviction of Paul, who cried out: "Woe to me if I do not preach the Gospel" (1 Cor 9:16).
>
> This passion will not fail to stir in the Church a new sense of mission, which cannot be left to a group of "specialists" but must involve the responsibility of all the members of the People of God. Those who have come into genuine contact with Christ cannot keep him for themselves, they must proclaim him. A new apostolic outreach

is needed, which will be lived as the everyday commitment of Christian communities and groups.[26]

The missionary mandate accompanies us into the Third Millennium and urges us to share the enthusiasm of the very first Christians: we can count on the power of the same Spirit who was poured out at Pentecost and who impels us still today to start out anew, sustained by the hope "which does not disappoint" (Rom 5:5).[27]

Pope Benedict XVI

Pope Benedict XVI has continued the theme of the need for a new Pentecost if our hopes for a new evangelization are to be realized. One of Pope Benedict XVI's first initiatives upon being elected pope was to call another meeting of the "new movements and communities" as a follow-up to the significant 1998 gathering convened by Pope John Paul II. His concluding prayer: "Let us pray to God the Father, therefore, through our Lord Jesus Christ, in the grace of the Holy Spirit, so that the celebration of the Solemnity of Pentecost may be like an ardent flame and a blustering wind for Christian life and for the mission of the whole Church.... Upon all of you I invoke an outpouring of the gifts of the Spirit, so that in our time too, we may have the experience of a renewed Pentecost. Amen!"[28]

Pope Benedict XVI has not only called for a "renewed Pentecost" but has called for a "culture of Pentecost" to be established in the Church.[29]

He also frequently identifies the mission of Jesus as to "baptize in the Holy Spirit."

On the Feast of the Baptism of the Lord on January 13, 2008, in connection with his administering the sacrament of Baptism, he declared:

Jesus was revealed as the One who came to baptize humanity in the Holy spirit: he came to give men and women life in abundance (cr. Jn 10:10), eternal life, which brings the human being back to life and heals him entirely, in body and in spirit, restoring him to the original plan for which he was created.[30]

Later that day he elaborated:

Christ's entire mission is summed up in this: to baptize us in the Holy Spirit, to free us from the slavery of death and "to open heaven to us," that is, access to the true and full life that will be a "plunging ever anew into the vastness of being, in which we are simply overwhelmed with joy" (*Spe Salvi*, n. 12).[31]

At the World Youth Day in Australia in 2008 he proclaimed:

Together we shall invoke the Holy Spirit, confidently asking God for the gift of a new Pentecost for the Church and for humanity in the third millennium.[32]

In reflecting on the text from Acts in which Jesus promises his disciples that they will be baptized in the Spirit, he invited not only youth but the whole Church: "Today I would like to extend this invitation to everyone: Let us rediscover, dear brothers and sisters, the beauty of being baptized in the Holy Spirit; let us be aware again of our Baptism and of our Confirmation, sources of grace that are always present. Let us ask the Virgin Mary to obtain a renewed Pentecost for the Church again today, a Pentecost that will spread in everyone the joy of living and witnessing to the Gospel."[33]

Certainly it can't be claimed that Pope Benedict XVI, by using the biblical terminology of baptism in the Holy Spirit, is asking everyone to be baptized in the Holy Spirit as it is understood and practiced in the Catholic charismatic renewal. It must be acknowledged, though, that he is making a very strong call to a renewal of the graces of Baptism and Confirmation in relationship to the event of Pentecost and its substance, which is described by Jesus as being "baptized in the Spirit." It must also be acknowledged that Pope Benedict XVI is perfectly aware of the use of this terminology to describe what the Catholic charismatic renewal calls baptism in the Spirit.

Upon his arrival in the United States on the occasion of his first visit as pope he strongly called for a "new outpouring of the Spirit."

> In the exercise of my ministry as the Successor of Peter, I have come to America to confirm you, my brothers and sisters, in the faith of the Apostles (cf. Lk 22:32). I have come to proclaim anew, as Peter proclaimed on the day of Pentecost, that Jesus Christ is Lord and Messiah, risen from the dead, seated in glory at the right hand of the Father, and established as judge of the living and the dead (cf. Acts 2:14ff.). I have come to repeat the Apostle's urgent call to conversion and the forgiveness of sins, and to implore from the Lord a new outpouring of the Holy Spirit upon the Church in this country.[34]

Later on the same visit, in St. Patrick's Cathedral in New York City, he even more emphatically proclaimed:

> Let us implore from God the grace of a new Pentecost for the Church in America. May tongues of fire, combining burning love of God and neighbor with zeal for the spread of Christ's Kingdom, descend on all present![35]

A New Pentecost: Why Now?

How to summarize the continuing papal calls for a New Pentecost? It seems to be based on two main perceptions. One perception is of the weakness of the Church and the "collapse of

Christendom" or as Pope John Paul II put it, the end of Christian society as we once knew it. This is related to the growth of an international, secular culture characterized by a "dictatorship of relativism," which is increasingly hostile to claims of truth and most especially the claims of Christ and the Church. A situation has now developed that is more similar to the situation the early Church faced than anything we've known in many centuries.

The second perception is that what is most needed is a renewal of a personal relationship with God himself, a relationship that "comes alive" in the reality of Pentecost, in both its contemplative and charismatic dimensions. Quite bluntly, it appears that the popes are crying out: we need God! We need a new Pentecost! This is in turn opening us to the perception that indeed, God is hearing our prayers and that we are beginning to see the unfolding of a new Pentecost, most notably in various renewal movements, but hopefully extending in an ever-widening circle to the entire Church. Pentecost and the gifts of the Spirit are not the property of any one movement or all the movements together, but the heritage of the entire Church. The movements perhaps can be seen as a "vanguard" of the renewal the Lord has in mind for the whole Church. The values and realities we see embodied in the movements and new communities are intended to stimulate the renewal of such values and realities throughout the Church.

Baptism in the Spirit: Preliminary Observations

It's been more than forty-five years since the charismatic renewal in the Catholic Church first appeared and nearly that long since the first attempts to theologically understand the core experience of this renewal — "baptism in the Holy Spirit" — from a Catholic point of view.

"Baptism in the Spirit" is the main terminology used in North America to describe an experience of the Spirit that is often accompanied by a deeper personal encounter with Christ. It is char-

acterized by a glimpse of his Lordship and an experience of the
Father's love that is personal and deeply liberating. And it evokes
a new awareness that we are truly not orphans but that the Holy
Spirit is truly present and ready to encourage, convict, guide, and
help us understand the things of God. This vital experience of
the Trinity brings with it a new or renewed desire for prayer, including in a special way, praise, adoration, and thanksgiving, a
new or renewed desire to read the Scripture, often described as
"the Scriptures coming alive" and a desire to tell others about the
goodness of God. A desire to be in relationship with other Christians frequently accompanies being baptized in the Spirit. And It
often involves the manifestation of one or more of the charisms
listed in 1 Corinthians 12, 1 Peter 4, and Romans 12. Fr. Francis
Sullivan offers this as a brief definition of the experience:

> A religious experience which initiates a decisively new
> sense of the powerful presence and working of God in
> one's life, which working usually involves one or more
> charismatic gifts.[36]

Cardinal Paul Cordes, recently retired president of the Pontifical Council Cor Unum, offers this description:

> "Baptism in the Holy Spirit" is a concrete experience of
> the "Grace of Pentecost," in which the working of the Holy
> Spirit becomes an experienced reality in the life of the
> individual and of the faith community. The experience
> of "Baptism in the Holy Spirit" is the certain and some-
> times overwhelming "realization" of the loving nearness
> of God.... It is a threshold of spiritual life that is crossed,
> bringing trust in the Father and a desire to being open to
> the teaching of the Holy Spirit ... making possible the per-
> ception of God's effective presence. This experiential per-
> ception reveals God in His immense incomprehensibility
> as well as in His loving and Fatherly care. This revelation
> of God attracts, opens new categories of thought, reveals

new goals and desires, makes clear the significance of God's will as well as of human sinfulness and the need for repentance.... It is, in short, the experiential rediscovery, in faith, that Jesus is Lord by the power of the Spirit to the glory of the Father.... It is an opening up, and unfolding of Trinitarian life in the baptized.[37]

Cardinal Suenens, for example, one of the main leaders of Vatican II, was living a very dedicated life, and his episcopal motto was *In Spiritu Sancto*. And yet he tells of the change that happened in him when he was prayed with for a greater release of the Holy Spirit in his life.

I did not discover the Holy Spirit through the Renewal. As I have said, the Spirit had long been at the center of my life.... I saw how some Christians live, who took the Acts of the Apostles at its word, and this led me to question the depth and the genuineness of my own faith. As a result, I found that I believed in the action of the Holy Spirit, but in a limited sphere; in me the Spirit could not call forth from the organ all the melody he wished; some of the pipes did not function, because they had not been used.

He continues to list the specific changes he experienced.[38]

Fr. Cantalamessa, Preacher to the Papal Household, tells of his struggle to open to another dimension of the Spirit's working, given his dedication as a son of St. Francis, his theological understanding as a university professor, the graces of priesthood, his already having received the Spirit in many ways. Eventually, it was noticing that Jesus humbled himself in asking for Baptism from John the Baptist "who was just a layman!" that overcame his resistances. He describes his decision to pray for "a new outpouring of the Spirit" as a "conscious renewal of my Baptism ... surrendering the reins of my life to Christ." His book is a theological analysis of the experience and its fruits in a person's life.[39]

It has been understood from the very first Catholic charismatic theological reflection, in 1969, that the term "baptism in the Spirit" had its primary referent in the giving of the Spirit that we see described in several places in the Acts of the Apostles. For the early Church, this Pentecostal outpouring was understood as normally experienced in the sacraments of Christian initiation. But in the contemporary situation many initiated Catholics — those who have received Baptism, Confirmation, and the Eucharist — need to encounter in a more experiential manner the graces of the sacraments. In order to make this clear, the earliest charismatic theologians recommended speaking of a "renewal of baptism in the Spirit."[40] By this they wanted to communicate their acknowledgment of the validity of the sacraments of initiation that Catholics have received and at the same time to communicate that more could and should be expected to be experienced.

Any terminology has its problems. Speaking of the "renewal" of baptism in the Spirit emphasizes that the Spirit has already been given in the sacraments but perhaps doesn't as clearly communicate that what the New Testament describes as happening hasn't yet happened for many Catholics today. Speaking simply though of "baptism in the Spirit" runs the risk of neglecting the fact that this grace is rooted in the sacraments of initiation. The terminology discussion will go on!

Let's now take a look now at some of the main Scripture texts that refer to the experience of being baptized in the Holy Spirit.

Baptism in the Spirit in Scripture

John the Baptist declares Jesus will "baptize in the Holy Spirit"

In all four of the Gospels (Mt 3:1–12; Mk 1:1–8; Lk 3:3–18; Jn 1:22–34) John the Baptist introduces Jesus as the one who will baptize in the Holy Spirit. Pope Benedict XVI identifies the event of Pentecost as "the 'Baptism in the Holy Spirit,'" which had been announced by John the Baptist and promised by Jesus. Jesus' "whole mission was aimed at giving the Spirit of God to men … in a superabundant way, like a waterfall able to purify every heart, to extinguish the flames of evil and ignite the fire of divine love in the world. The Acts of the Apostles present Pentecost as a fulfillment of such a promise and therefore as the crowning moment of Jesus' whole mission."[41]

Jesus' post-Resurrection instructions

Jesus, in a post resurrection appearance, interprets the Scriptures to his disciples, explaining that it was necessary that "the Messiah would suffer and rise from the dead on the third day and that repentance, for the forgiveness of sins, would be preached in his name to all the nations." He tells them, though, not to undertake the mission until they receive the "promise of my Father upon you; but stay in the city until you are clothed with power from on high" (Lk 24:44–47, 49).

Luke recounts, in the Acts of the Apostles, that just before Jesus ascended to the Father, completing his post-resurrection appearances, he instructed the disciples, again, "not to depart from Jerusalem, but to wait for 'the promise of the Father about which you have heard me speak; for John baptized with water, but in a few days you will be baptized with the Holy Spirit.'" The disciples' response was typical, asking Jesus if the time had arrived for him to restore Israel's independence under their own king. Jesus, also typically doesn't directly answer their question, discouraging their eschatological curiosity, but underlines the importance of their paying attention to what he has just told them. "It is not for you to know the times or seasons that the Father has established by his own authority. But you will receive power when the Holy Spirit comes upon you, and you will be my witnesses in Jerusalem, throughout Judea and Samaria, and to the ends of the earth" (Acts 1:1–12).

The Pentecost event and Peter's interpretation

On the Jewish feast of Pentecost, originally a "first fruits" harvest festival, the disciples were praying in an "upper room" when the remarkable Pentecost event happened. The outward manifestations of the sound of a driving wind and the appearance of flames of fire signaled a profound interior experience that expressed itself in bold preaching. A multilingual crowd miraculously were able to hear what the disciples were saying each in their own languages. Raniero Cantalamessa, echoing multiple fathers of the Church, describes this inspired proclamation of the "mighty acts of God" as a "sober intoxication."[42]

Luke gives an insight into what the scene must have been like by recording the interpretation of some whom had gathered that the apostles "have had too much new wine" (Acts 2:1–4, 12).

Peter then stands up and denies that they are drunk with wine. (Paul would later exhort the Christians in Ephesus: "do not get drunk on wine … but be filled with the Spirit" [Eph 5:18].) And he explains that what they "see and hear" is nothing less than the fulfillment of the entire Old Testament preparation of God's people for the Messiah.

Pentecost is the name of the feast day on which the "event" of the disciples being baptized in the Spirit happened. Pentecost was the occasion; baptism in the Spirit is the term used by Jesus and the apostles for the substance of what happened.

The Extension of Baptism in the Spirit

Samaria

Luke now develops the theme that the apostles expect each new convert to come into the same experience of being baptized in the Spirit as the disciples themselves each did on the feast of Pentecost. When word reached the apostles that "Samaria had accepted the word of God," they sent Peter and John who "prayed for them, that they might receive the Holy spirit, for it had not yet fallen upon any of them; they had only been baptized in the name of the Lord Jesus. Then they laid hands on them and they received the Holy Spirit." Luke points out that when Simon "saw that the Spirit was conferred by the laying on of the apostles' hands," he sought to pay for the secret of being able to do this (Acts 8:14–19). In the "Samaritan Pentecost" as with the initial "Pentecost" there are visible signs of the Spirit's coming, charismatic manifestations, unspecified in this instance, which cause bystanders to marvel.

Cornelius and his household

By means of divine guidance Peter is led to the home of Cornelius, a Roman God-fearer, who also has been prepared by the Spirit to receive his visit and message. Peter explains the saving deeds of Christ to Cornelius. While he is still speaking, "the Holy Spirit fell upon all who were listening to the word." The Jewish Christians who were with Peter "were astounded that the gift of the Holy Spirit should have been poured out on the Gentiles, also, for they could hear them speaking in tongues and glorifying God." Peter then declares that they should be baptized because they "have received the Holy Spirit even as we have." What happened to the disciples on the day of Pentecost, being baptized in the Spirit, happens now to Cornelius and his household. Peter's assurance of the appropriateness of baptizing these Gentiles rests on perceiving, through visible indicators — speaking in tongues and glorifying God — that they have been baptized in the Spirit just as the apostles have been. This, of course, is an indication that Jesus is present again, baptizing in the Spirit (Acts 10:44–48).

Peter, understandably, is criticized for baptizing Gentiles. In his defense he describes the manifest "falling" of the Holy Spirit on the Gentiles, an experience that he could not deny; and then he recalls the theological explanation: "I remembered the word of the Lord, how he had said, 'John baptized with water but you will be baptized with the Holy Spirit.'" Peter then declares that if God has given "the same gift" to the Gentiles that he gave to the Jewish Christians, how could he hinder what God was doing. The criticism turned to praise as Peter's colleagues acknowledged that God indeed had decided to grant "life-giving repentance to the Gentiles too" as they were obviously baptized in the Spirit just as the apostles had been (Acts 11:15–18).

Ephesus

Paul encounters a group of "disciples" in Ephesus but must have noticed that something was missing in their experience of God. He asks them if they had received the Holy Spirit when they became believers. He discovers that they have never even heard about the Holy Spirit but have simply been baptized with the baptism for repentance of John the Baptist. Paul explains that John was simply preparing the way for Jesus and baptizes them in the name of Jesus. "When Paul laid his hands on them, the Holy Spirit came upon them, and they spoke in tongues and prophesied" (Acts 19:1–7). Paul "fills in the picture" for these well-meaning but insufficiently evangelized and catechized "disciples," which enables them to be joined to Jesus through Baptism and filled with the Spirit. Again, there are tangible signs that normally accompany being baptized in the Spirit. In this instance speaking in tongues and prophesying are noted. All these accounts in Acts of the Apostles reflect the Apostles' persistent concern that each new group of converts come into the same experience of the Spirit as they did on the day of Pentecost. Sometimes it is noted that these events are in the context of "new horizons" that are opening up for the spread of the gospel and perhaps the "same experience" should not be expected in other, less significant, circumstances. Such observations overlook the whole witness of Acts and the epistles to numerous Christian communities living a life characterized by a "culture of Pentecost" well beyond the specific incidents of initiation recounted in Acts. To cite just one:

O stupid Galatians! Who has bewitched you, before whose eyes Jesus Christ was publicly portrayed as crucified? I want to learn only this from you: did you receive the Spirit from works of the law, or from faith in what you heard? Are you so stupid? After beginning with the Spirit, are you now ending with the flesh? Did you experience so many things in vain? — if indeed it was in vain. Does, then, the one who supplies the Spirit to you and works mighty deeds among you do so from works of the law or from faith in what you heard? (Gal 3:1–5)

Repeated fillings with the Spirit

As opposition rises against the believers (which includes harsh threats, beatings, and actual imprisonments), they confidently ask God for the boldness and supernatural power necessary to carry out their mission in the face of such opposition. "'And now Lord, take note of their threats, and enable your servants to speak your word with all boldness, as you stretch forth your hand to heal, and signs and wonders are done through the name of your holy servant Jesus.' As they prayed, the place where they were gathered shook, and they were all filled with the Holy Spirit and continued to speak the word of God with boldness" (Acts 4:23–33).

As almost 1,700 years of Christendom collapses and a new international pagan culture gains the ascendency, even rising to that "dictatorship of relativism" that Pope Benedict XVI warns us about, the Church in the West is encountering circumstances that are more like those encountered by the early Church than anything we've known in our lifetimes. The recent popes' consistent calls for a new Pentecost as being perhaps the deepest need of the Church today, surely can only be advanced by a deeper theological understanding of what many millions have experienced as baptism in the Holy Spirit.

And as Fr. Kilian McDonnell has graciously and wisely said:

Whether the release of the Spirit is due to an awakening of sacramental grace or merely the fruit of prayer, the important thing is that it *happen*.[43]

Let's pray that it "happens" for us and for the whole Church.[44]

Lord, I want more of your Holy Spirit. Activate aspects of His work that have been dormant in my life. Bring me into a deeper relationship with you. Give me greater zeal to be a witness for you and live a life of prayer, love, and service. Pour out your Holy Spirit on the whole Church! We need you Lord! Come!

Chapter V

What Is the Message?

In chapter II we focused in a particular way on the question of the eternal destinies of those who haven't had a chance to hear the Gospel and looked closely at the much neglected teaching of *Lumen gentium* 16. In this and the subsequent chapter we will look at the situation of those who do hear the Gospel. What kind of response is necessary for the saving grace of the Gospel to become effective in a hearer's life? Let's begin by looking closely at the basic gospel message.

John 3:16, that short summary of the gospel that is commonly seen on signs at sports events, as we have already noted, accurately summarizes the gospel:

> Yes, God so loved the world that he gave his only Son, that whoever believes in him may not die but may have eternal life. (Jn 3:16)

Often overlooked in this text is the clear implication that not believing in Jesus means perishing. Believing or not believing, responding to the Father's love or not responding, has eternal consequences. This is why it matters so much that we respond to the call to evangelization. The eternal destinies of people we love are at stake.

Let's look at a somewhat longer text (Eph 2:1–10) that brings out in a striking way the reason we have to be thankful that God has given us his only Son:

> You were dead because of your sins and offenses, as you gave allegiance to the present age and to the prince of the

air, that spirit who is even now at work among the rebel-
lious. All of us were once of their company; we lived at the
level of the flesh, following every whim and fancy, and so
by nature deserved God's wrath like the rest. But God is
rich in mercy; because of his great love for us he brought
us to life with Christ when we were dead in sin. By this
favor you were saved. Both with and in Christ Jesus he
raised us up and gave us a place in the heavens, that in the
ages to come he might display the great wealth of his favor, manifested by his kindness to us in Christ Jesus. (Eph
2:1–7)

Only when we realize what our situation apart from Christ is
can we adequately appreciate the great gift of salvation. Our sins
and offenses, our allegiance to a world in rebellion against God,
our openness to the workings of the evil one — all put us in a situation that causes spiritual death, now and eternally. Our sin and
alienation from God also consigns us to a superficial life. Thus we
live at the level of disordered desires and at the mercy of our own
foolishness. We are victimized by the principalities and powers
working through the world structures of fashion, entertainment,
supposed sophistication, economics, false beliefs, and destructive
behavior. This passage brings out the really shocking truth that
because of all of this we deserve God's wrath.

Because of our participation in the sin of the world we are
spiritually dead, incapable of relationship with God, and destined
for hell. We rarely hear the truth of sin, hell, the power of the
devil, and the just wrath of God spoken of today. But that doesn't
make these realities any less true. Even if many of our fellow
Catholics believe that almost everybody will be saved and hardly
anyone will end up in hell, that doesn't change the truth of Jesus'
merciful words of warning:

"Enter through the narrow gate. The gate that leads to
damnation is wide, the road is clear, and many choose to
travel it. But how narrow is the gate that leads to life, how

rough the road, and how few there are who find it!" (Mt 7:13–14)

The really good news is that even though apart from Christ we deserve hell, we are offered instead the chance for heaven. And those currently on the broad way leading to destruction don't have to stay on that road. If we accept the sacrifice Christ offered on our behalf, for the remission of our sin, which implies faith, repentance, and baptism, we can be saved. Let's look at the text from Ephesians again.

> … and so by nature deserved God's wrath like the rest. But God is rich in mercy; because of his great love for us he brought us to life with Christ when we were dead in sin. By this favor you were saved.

Even though apart from Christ we deserve God's wrath, God in his mercy because of his great love for us offers Christ to us as provision for our sin and as the doorway to heaven, if we respond in faith and live in accordance with him. It is by God's favor that we are offered the possibility of salvation.

This is such an important part of the basic good news that Paul repeats it so that he is sure we don't misunderstand the significance of what he is saying.

> I repeat, it is owing to his favor that salvation is yours through faith. This is not your own doing, it is God's gift; neither is it a reward for anything you have accomplished, so let no one pride himself on it. (Eph 2:8–9)

Paul doesn't want us to miss the pure act of gratuitous love of the Father's gift of Jesus to us. He makes it clear that the salvation offered to us in Jesus is not our own doing in any way, nor is it a reward for anything we have accomplished.

The reason why God has established his plan of salvation in this manner is precisely so that no one can "pride himself on it."

And here's the nub of the question. The original sin that besets our race was rooted in the sin of unbelief and pride. The appeal of the evil one to our first parents was first to undermine confidence in the truthfulness and goodness of God and his Word. The evil one flatly contradicted the Word of God: "You will not die, for God knows that when you eat of it your eyes will be opened, and you will be like God, knowing good and evil." Withdrawing the mind and heart from confidence in God and the truthfulness of his word — the sin of unbelief — led to direct disobedience, to the darkening of mind and heart, and the corruption of human nature that issued in death. Only when we crucify our desire to be independent from God through faith, conversion, and baptism, and humbly accept our status as creatures dependent on God for everything can we be saved. This requires repentance from unbelief and a return to trust in God and obedience to his will, which is our happiness. As we share this word of love and truth in evangelization, God gives the grace of faith and repentance so that people may not die but have eternal life.

Fr. Francis Martin expresses this truth in a striking manner:

> The root sin of the world is refusal to believe in Jesus and the place he holds next to the Father as the Revelation of the Father, the root sin is to reject the Truth. "Whoever believes in the Son has eternal life, whoever disobeys the Son will not see life, but must endure God's wrath." (Jn 3:36).[45]

Salvation then, in its first moments, is not something we achieve, but something we humbly and gratefully receive through faith and trust in the merciful words and deeds of the Lord. We are saved most especially by the sacrificial death of Jesus on the cross and his glorious resurrection, ascension, and pouring out of the Holy Spirit, and his final coming to judge the living and the dead.

Genuine conversion and faith issue in "works" — prayer, holiness, good deeds, loving service, patient suffering, works of mercy and evangelism, actions in favor of peace and justice. And these very works are themselves made possible in us through ongoing grace and faith. The works themselves are gifts from God; the power and desire to do them are also gifts from God. As the concluding part of the text from Ephesians we are considering says:

> We are truly his handiwork, created in Christ Jesus to lead the life of good deeds which God prepared for us in advance. (Eph 2:10)

Another important summary of the gospel that Paul gives is classically called the *kerygma* — the basic message of the deeds of Christ that are the foundation of our salvation.

> For I delivered to you as of first importance what I also received, that Christ died for our sins in accordance with the Scriptures, that he was buried, that he was raised on the third day in accordance with the Scriptures, and that he appeared to Cephas, then to the twelve. Then he appeared to more than five hundred brethren at one time, most of whom are still alive, though some have fallen asleep. Then he appeared to James, then to all the apostles. Last of all, as to one untimely born, he appeared also to me. (1 Cor 15:3–8)

A sacrifice was needed to reconcile God and man, an atonement for sin. And the God-man Jesus in an unfathomable act of love offered his life for our salvation and opened a path to friendship with God and eternal life. If we respond in faith, repentance, and baptism to his offering, and become united to him in his atoning death and in his glorious resurrection, we too will share eternal life with him. Our eternal life will begin now in the outpouring of the Holy Spirit and the Eucharistic life of the Church. It will find its full flowering in our own resurrection from the dead to the glory of heaven when Jesus comes again in glory to judge the living and the dead.

Mercy must be received

There has been a tremendous stress on the infinite mercy of God in contemporary Catholicism. It's based of course on Divine Revelation, but made a central focus due to the wide promulgation of the moving communications that St. Faustina received from the Lord, which have been recognized by the Church as of a high order of reliability. The papal endorsement of St. Faustina, culminating in her canonization and then the institution of the Feast of Divine Mercy, has brought the message of mercy front and center in the Church. And millions have benefitted in increased confidence, hope, and devotion.

But, the devil, always looking for a way to deceive God's people and divert them from the true path of salvation, has found a way to turn this emphasis on mercy to his own evil purposes. Important parts of St. Faustina's revelations are generally being ignored, which has led to a dangerous presumption on God's mercy. It is not uncommon to hear people say that "God is so merciful" that maybe only people like Hitler will be lost and that everybody else will be "okay."

As we have seen in our examination of *Lumen gentium* 16, telling half the truth can create a lie. Just as ignoring the last three sentences of the conciliar text has contributed to massive deception, so too ignoring the whole context and content of St. Faustina's communication of the depths of Divine Mercy has contributed to the very same deception.

The Lord regularly tells St. Faustina that she is to be a messenger preparing the way for his Second Coming and Final Judgment. While he extends mercy to the whole human race now, the time of judgment is coming when he will judge people on the basis of their response — or lack of response — to mercy. Those who presume on the mercy of God without repenting are "storing up wrath" for themselves.

> Do you presume upon the riches of his kindness and forbearance and patience? Do you not know that God's kind-

ness is meant to lead you to repentance? But by your hard and impenitent heart you are storing up wrath for yourselves on the day of wrath when God's righteous judgment will be revealed. For he will render to every man according to his works: to those who by patience in well-doing seek for glory and honor and immortality, he will give eternal life, but for those who are factious and do not obey the truth, but obey wickedness, there will be wrath and fury. (Rom 2:4–8)

This, of course, however little averred to today, is the message we have been commanded by Christ to proclaim as well.

"And he commanded us to preach to the people, and to testify that he is the one ordained by God to be judge of the living and the dead. To him all the prophets bear witness that everyone who believes in him receives forgiveness of sins through his name." (Acts 10:42–43)

Despite the immense mercy of God it is apparent from the message that many are nevertheless in danger of being lost, and some will definitely be lost. Whether more will be saved or lost and the exact meaning of "many" is not revealed, but the realities revealed to St. Faustina are sobering. For example:

Jesus looked at me and said, Souls perish in spite of My bitter Passion. I am giving them the last hope of salvation; that is the Feast of My Mercy. If they will not adore My mercy, they will perish for all eternity. Secretary of My mercy, write, tell souls about this great mercy of mine, because the awful day, the day of My justice, is near.[46]

Some people have, mistakenly, gotten the impression from the helpful emphasis on mercy that sin is no big deal and that God in His mercy will never allow anyone to be lost. This is not at all what the Scripture and Church teach, nor is it what the Lord showed to St. Faustina.

St. Faustina's Description of Hell

During St. Faustina's eight-day retreat in 1936 an angel led her through hell, and she describes what she saw and relates that the Lord told her to write it down.

> Today, I was led by an Angel to the chasms of hell. It is a place of great torture; how awesomely large and extensive it is! The kinds of tortures I saw: the first torture that constitutes hell is the loss of God; the second is perpetual remorse of conscience; the third is that one's condition will never change; the fourth is the fire that will penetrate the soul without destroying it — a terrible suffering, since it is a purely spiritual fire, lit by God's anger; the fifth torture is continual darkness and a terrible suffocating smell, and, despite the darkness, the devils and the souls of the damned see each other and all the evil, both of others and their own; the sixth torture is the constant company of Satan; the seventh torture is horrible despair, hatred of God, vile words, curses, and blasphemies. These are the tortures suffered by all the damned together, but that is not the end of the sufferings. There are special tortures destined for particular souls. These are the torments of the senses. Each soul undergoes terrible and indescribable sufferings, related to the manner in which it has sinned. There are caverns and pits of torture where one form of agony differs from another. I would have died at the very sight of these tortures if the omnipotence of God had not supported me. Let the sinner know that he will be tortured throughout all eternity, in those senses which he made use of to sin.[47]

Admittedly these are difficult descriptions to read. And indeed, the images used are referring to a reality that is hard to express in human words, and the use of the particular images almost certainly imperfectly conveys this reality. At the same time it must be recognized that Jesus himself used images such as "outer darkness" (Mt 22:13) where there will be weeping and gnashing of teeth; and "unquenchable fire" (Mk 9:43) or the "furnace of fire" (Mt 13; 42–50) or the "lake of fire" (Rev 20:15; 21:8). Or sometimes hell is described by Jesus as the place where the tormenting worm never stops gnawing (Mk 9:48). Jesus makes his own the fiery language of John the Baptist. In the profundity of the Last Supper Discourses he makes clear that "If a man does not abide in me, he is cast forth as a branch and withers; and the branches are gathered, thrown into the fire and burned" (Jn 15:6). And can we find stronger words than those of Jesus, which he tells us he will speak at the last judgment: "Depart from me, you cursed, into the eternal fire prepared for the devil and his angels.... And they will go away into eternal punishment, but the righteous into eternal life" (Mt 25:41, 46).

Some may wish to emphasize that sinners bring this separation from God and union with the demonic on themselves by their own choices. Others may say that these images may be weak human figures that imperfectly point to the horror of separation from God and may not need to be taken literally. Yet the shocking fact remains that St. Faustina is describing something that she believes God showed her precisely to warn sinners and call them to not presume on the mercy of God; and further, to ward off attempts to say that hell may exist but perhaps no one is there. Faustina continues:

> I am writing this at the command of God, so that no soul may find an excuse by saying there is no hell, or that nobody has ever been there, and so no one can say what it is like.
>
> I, Sister Faustina, by the order of God, have visited the abysses of hell so that I might tell souls about it and testify to its existence. I cannot speak about it now; but I have received a command from God to leave it in writing. The devils were full of hatred for me, but they had to obey me at the command of God. What I have written is but a

pale shadow of the things I saw. But I noticed one thing: that most of the souls there are those who disbelieved that there is a hell.[48]

St. Faustina saw her whole mission as a way of preparing God's people for the return of the Lord.

Now is the time when mercy is being extended to the world, but this time will come to an end and the Lord will return in glory to judge the living and the dead. And whether we are alive or not at the Lord's return, we need to be ready to meet him at any moment as no one knows the day or the hour, not only of the Lord's return but of the length of our own lives.

Almost seven hundred years earlier, the Lord gave to St. Catherine of Siena a virtually identical vision/insight into the inner realities of hell, purgatory, and heaven. We will only briefly summarize here what the Father showed her about hell and heaven.

St. Catherine of Siena's Vision of the Ultimate Destinations

The Father gave to Catherine a vivid understanding of the reality of hell, giving her an insight into the four principal sufferings that are undergone there, very similar to what the Lord showed St. Faustina almost six hundred years later.

The first suffering that God the Father communicates to Catherine is the agony of never being one with God. The second is bitter regret — not true repentance for sin — but the regret one sometimes encounters in prisoners who regret that they were caught, and regret the punishment but show no sorrow for the crime. The third suffering of hell is the oppositie of the beatific vision — the fulness of all delight in union with God in heaven — the demonic vision, seeing the devil as he truly is in all his perverse evil and malevolence. Now we know through the Sacred Scriptures that the devil disguises himself on this earth as an "angel of light," but the unfortunate souls in hell will see him as he truly is in all his horror and perversity.

The Father indicates that the lost souls in seeing the horrifying sight of the devil come to know themselves better and what they have become through their unrepented sin. Just as in life all knowledge of supernatural realities is significantly veiled, after death the veil is removed and both evil and good are seen for what they really are. By turning to Christ, we gradually become more like him in his great beauty; by turning to sin and the lies and deceptions of the devil, we become more like him in his extreme horror and ugliness. What we have become through the beliefs and actions we have given ourselves to in this life is revealed with utter clarity after death. As the Father expressed it to Catherine:

> Their suffering is even worse because they see the devil as he really is — more horrible than the human heart can imagine.

The Father then reminds Catherine of an experience she once had after being given a glimpse of the devil, how she said she would rather walk on a road of fire until the Day of Judgment than see him again. He then tells her, "Even with all you have seen you do not really know how horrible he is."

The fourth torment is the ceaseless burning of an immaterial fire that has as many forms as the forms of the sins that were committed and is more or less severe in proportion to their seriousness.[49]

The Fear of the Lord

The "fear of the Lord" as it is spoken of in the Bible is not just a concept, but an experience that predisposes us to wisdom. In fact, "The fear of the LORD is the beginning of wisdom; a good understanding have all those who practice it" (Ps 111:10; Sir 1:14).

This fear is not the fear of a tyrannical God who impetuously and arbitrarily inflicts punishment, but the proper respect, and fear, of a just God who administers just punishment for those who deserve it. Contemporary commentators are so eager to distinguish the fuller meaning of "fear of the Lord" from servile fear that they often eliminate the very healthy fear of eternal loss that is the sign of a realistic person. Yet Jesus himself told us that this indeed was a healthy and necessary fear to have.

> "And do not fear those who kill the body but cannot kill the soul; rather fear him who can destroy both soul and body in hell." (Mt 10:28)

We'd be foolish not to "fear the loss of heaven and the pains of hell," as a familiar Act of Contrition puts it.

The biblical fear of the Lord is an intelligent fear, based on a deep perception of the holiness and majesty of God. It rightly recognizes the possibility of violating the law of God, despising his love, rejecting his mercy, and meriting eternal separation from Him. While the fear of the Lord is simply the beginning of wisdom, and the end of wisdom is love (1 Jn 4:17), one doesn't jump to love without a deep, and ongoing, experience of biblical, Spirit-inspired fear. The Scripture tells us in fact that "blessed is the man who fears the LORD", and that, indeed, this God-given fear of the Lord frees us from other fears. "He is not afraid of evil news; his heart is firm, trusting in the LORD. His heart is steady, he will not be afraid" (Ps 112:1, 7–8).

> The fear of the Lord is glory and exaltation,
>   and gladness and a crown of rejoicing.
> The fear of the Lord delights the heart,
>   and gives gladness and joy and long life.
> With him who fears the Lord it will go well at the end;
>   on the day of his death he will be blessed. (Sir 1:11–13)

Today there is a great aversion to an appropriate "fear of the Lord." And consequently there is a great trivialization of love and a great foolishness as regards relationship with God. Fear of the Lord is a gift of God; it is not opposed to love, but prepares for it. Fear of the Lord and love of the Lord go together. One of the reasons why there has been so much foolishness in the Church and in the world is because there has been so much lack of fear of the Lord.

The Glory of Heaven

One of the things that is most striking as Catherine recounts what the Father is showing her is how much more "depth" there is to reality than many commonly suppose. Sin and evil are far uglier and more horrendous than most of us can imagine, but unimaginable too is the beauty, glory, and goodness of heaven. The Father shows Catherine that the joy and glory of heaven is beyond anything that we can imagine or hope for as we will share in the very glory of the risen Christ ourselves, in our risen bodies as well as in our souls. Freed from fear by the infusion of divine love in our souls we wait for divine judgment with gladness, not fear, having lived our life in love of God and neighbor.[50]

Bernard of Clairvaux, hundreds of years before Catherine, strikingly describes the difference in the ultimate destinations of human beings:

> Those who are in darkness will be in darkness still, and those who see will see more and more ... and this is the last day of both, complete blindness and perfect sight. Then nothing remains to be taken from those who are completely emptied, nor is there anything more to be given to those who are filled, unless they may expect to receive more than fullness, according to the promise made to them.... "They shall put into your arms full measure pressed down and overflowing" (Lk 6:38) ... a weight of glory (2 Cor 4:17) exalted above measure, so that the super abundant outpouring of light should reflect upon bodies

also ... those whom he enlightens within he adorns also without, and clothes them with a robe of glory (Sir 6:32).[51]

The union and love of God that begins in this life and grows as the spiritual journey progresses will be gloriously manifested and perfected in heaven. But so is the union and love that we have with one another in this life gloriously manifested and perfected in heaven. The Father tells Catherine that the particular relationships we had on earth, insofar as they were in the Lord, will actually increase in depth of intimacy and love in heaven. Friendships and marriages that are lived in and with Jesus will indeed be "saved" and indeed prove to be a love that is truly "forever." The time for biological procreation will have come to an end, our bodies now transformed in glory, made ready for an eternity of celebration, but the love, in Christ, that was built up in true Christian relationships will last forever. We will not only know and recognize one another in heaven, but know and love each other even more!

> And though they are all joined in the bond of charity, they know a special kind of sharing with those whom they loved most closely with a special love in the world, a love through which they grew in grace and virtue. They helped each other proclaim the glory and praise of my name in themselves and in their neighbors, So now in everlasting life they have not lost that love; no, they still love and share with other even more closely and fully, adding their love to the good of all ... when a soul reaches eternal life, all share in her good and she in theirs.[52]

Not only do souls know and love each other even more fully in heaven, but they don't stop knowing and loving people that are still on the journey on earth. We are not alone. We are known. We are loved. The Father tells Catherine that those already with him continually intercede for us who are still on the journey and that the Father will do everything to answer their prayer "provided only that you do not foolishly resist my mercy."[53]

There has been much silence, or outright skepticism, in the Church in recent decades concerning heaven and hell, the horror of sin and the glory of heaven. So it may be that confronting the vision of Catherine — which is absolutely scripturally based and firmly embedded in the tradition of the church — may cause us to struggle with issues of "fairness." And we may want to ask the famous question, "How could a good God send someone to hell?" It's interesting to note how the Father shows Catherine that as each person dies they actually rush to where they want to be. In a very real way each person chooses their own destiny over the course of a lifetime and at the moment of death embraces what has truly become their choice.

We Choose Our Own Destiny

How great is the stupidity of those who make themselves weak in spite of my strengthening, and put themselves into the devil's hands! I want you to know, then, that at the moment of death, because they have put themselves during life under the devil's rule (not by force, because they cannot be forced, as I told you; but they put themselves voluntarily into his hands), and because they come to the point of death under this perverse rule, they can expect no other judgment but that of their own conscience. They come without hope to eternal damnation. In hate they grasp at hell in the moment of their death, and even before they possess it, they take hell as their prize along with their lords the demons.[54]

As horrible as the final moments of unrepentant sinners are, so wonderful are the final moments of those who die trusting in the mercy of the Lord. The Father shows Catherine that souls that lived in love of God and neighbor during their lifetimes and die in that love, "trusting in the blood of the lamb," rush toward His love and are welcomed into eternal life. "And so they taste eternal life even before they have left their mortal bodies."

Even Purgatory makes perfect sense and is revealed as a marvelous provision of God's mercy, a wonderful part of the Good News. Those who die in friendship with Christ but still needed purification know that is what they need and gladly go to the place of purification, trusting in the Lord's mercy to make them ready for heaven.

Catherine summarizes the Father's words:

> So no one waits to be judged. All receive their appointed place as they leave this life. They taste it and possess it even before they leave their bodies at the moment of death: the damned in hate and despair; the perfect in love, with the light of faith and trusting in the blood. And the imperfect, in mercy and with the same faith, come to that place called purgatory.[55]

The state of our soul even determines how the Lord "appears" to us and what emotion the encounter with him instills in us. As Bernard puts it:

> You see, the gaze of the Lord, though ever in itself unchanged, does not always produce the same effect. It conforms to each person's deserts, inspiring some with fear but bringing solace and security to others.[56]

The Father reveals to Catherine a very similar insight.[57]

Even in this life the condition of our soul will color how we think of and perceive God.

Part of Catherine's special mission as a Doctor of the Church is to teach the biblical worldview that is found in the Scripture, augmented by the particular insights that the Father gives her for this purpose. It was Catherine's burning awareness of the biblical worldview and the reality of the ultimate destinations that moved her with such energy to evangelize. But this worldview, in all its essentials is shared by a veritable "cloud of witnesses" across the centuries of Doctors and Saints and the countless "little ones" whom the Lord is so delighted to welcome into the Kingdom. They bring to light for each generation the seriousness of the situation of the human race apart from Christ; the reality of heaven and hell and the urgent necessity to order one's life right now as much as possible to the following of Jesus. As Bernard bluntly puts it:

> Lord Jesus, whoever refuses to live for you is clearly worthy of death, and is in fact dead already. Whoever does not know you is a fool. And whoever wants to become something without you, without doubt that man is considered nothing and is just that.... You have made all things for yourself, O God, and whoever wants to live for himself and not for you, in all that he does, is nothing. "Fear God, and keep his commandments," it is said, "for this is the whole duty of man" (Eccl 12:13).[58]

Chapter VI

What Response to Mercy Is Necessary for Salvation?

We must know we need mercy in order to receive it. We must realize that we are not "okay" as we are or by our own efforts. Admitting our need for mercy implies confessing our sins and asking forgiveness. It implies turning in faith and repentance toward the loving mercy of God. It also implies a redirection of our life toward the merciful Jesus, believing in him, obeying him, receiving his teachings, becoming his disciple, being nourished in the Eucharistic participation in his body and blood.

The Necessity of Faith

We have already briefly commented on the importance of faith in order to have eternal life and not to perish. But we now need to recognize just how emphatically Scripture stresses the absolute necessity of faith in order to be saved.

When people asked Jesus, "What must we do, to be doing the works of God?" Jesus told them, "This is the work of God, that you believe in him whom he has sent" (Jn 6:28–29).

In addition, Scripture warns that to refuse to believe in Jesus destines us for condemnation (hell).

This is starkly stated in the well-known ending of Mark's Gospel:

> And he said to them, "Go into all the world and preach the gospel to the whole creation. He who believes and is baptized will be saved; but he who does not believe will be condemned." (Mk 16:15–16)

Pope Francis lovingly repeated this basic truth during his first Good Friday Way of the Cross comments at the Coliseum: "… in judging us, God loves us. If I embrace his love then I am saved, if I refuse it, then I am condemned."

The consistent message of Scripture, unmistakably clear in the teachings of Jesus and the Apostles is that not to respond with faith, repentance, and baptism to the truth that the Gospel announces is to be condemned.

Immediately following the famous text of Jn 3:16 that we have previously commented on we find an even more striking statement of the truth of the necessity of response.

> For God sent the Son into the world, not to condemn the world, but that the world might be saved through him. He who believes in him is not condemned; he who does not believe is condemned already, because he has not believed in the name of the only begotten Son of God. (Jn 3:17–18)

Immediately before Jn 3:16 we find another strong affirmation of the necessity of faith in order to have eternal life.

> "No one has ascended into heaven but he who descended from heaven, the Son of man. And as Moses lifted up the serpent in the wilderness, so must the Son of man be lifted up, that whoever believes in him may have eternal life." (Jn 3:13–15)

And this light-filled chapter concludes:

> He who believes in the Son has eternal life; he who does not obey the Son shall not see life, but the wrath of God rests upon him. (Jn 3:36)

This is the consistent teaching of Jesus:

> "For this is the will of my Father, that everyone who sees the Son and believes in him should have eternal life; and I will raise him up at the last day.... Truly, truly, I say to you, he who believes has eternal life. I am the bread of life.... If anyone eats of this bread, he will live forever; and the bread which I shall give for the life of the world is my flesh." (Jn 6:40, 47–50)

> "I am the door; if any one enters by me, he will be saved, and will go in and out and find pasture. The thief comes only to steal and kill and destroy; I came that they may have life and have it abundantly. I am the good shepherd.... My sheep hear my voice, and I know them, and they follow me; and I give them eternal life, and they shall never perish, and no one shall snatch them out of my hand...." The Jews took up stones again to stone him. (Jn 10:9–11, 27–31)

And this is clearly the understanding of the Apostles:

> But when the Jews saw the multitudes, they were filled with jealousy, and contradicted what was spoken by Paul, and reviled him. And Paul and Barnabas spoke out boldly, saying, "It was necessary that the word of God should be spoken first to you. Since you thrust it from you, and judge yourselves unworthy of eternal life, behold, we turn to the Gentiles." ... And when the Gentiles heard this, they were glad and glorified the word of God; and as many as were ordained to eternal life believed. (Acts 13:45–48)

Unworthy of Eternal Life?

It might be well to make a few comments here about those who are "ordained" or destined (as other translations put it) to eternal life, and those who are "unworthy of eternal life" or "destined" to destruction. A text in Second Thessalonians helps us understand what this means. Paul is reminding the Thessalonians about his teaching on the second coming and final judgment. He assures them that this will not take place until certain conditions are fulfilled. He mentions that the Lord will not return until the "mass apostasy" or "rebellion" happens and until a restrainer on the work of evil and lawlessness is removed and unrestrained evil sweeps the world. His description of this event gives us insight into who is "destined" or ordained to be saved and lost:

> The coming of the lawless one by the activity of Satan will be with all power and with pretended signs and wonders, and with all wicked deception for those who are to perish, because they refused to love the truth and so be saved. Therefore God sends upon them a strong delusion, to make them believe what is false, so that all may be condemned who did not believe the truth but had pleasure in unrighteousness. (2 Thess 2:9–12)

Those who are destined for salvation are those who love the truth. Those who are destined for condemnation are those who did not believe the truth but gave themselves over to immorality. It's almost as if the devil will be permitted to "reap" what belongs to him before the Lord returns and judges the living and the dead and destroys this final, unrestrained manifestation of evil at his second coming. Here we are touching on the mystery of human freedom. God in his unfathomable wisdom has decreed that there be a genuine core of human freedom in the heart of each person that makes possible the reality of actual friendship and love. Love and friendship that is "forced" in any way is not real love or friendship. That's why, on the human level, if there is any compulsion in a marriage there are clear grounds for annulment — a declaration that a valid marriage never existed. God is looking for what is virtually inconceivable to the fallen human mind — genuine friendship with God, even in the mysterious words of Peter "participation in the divine nature." God is not looking for robots or slaves. He is offering friendship — as amazing as that is. This means that there is the genuine possibility of a "no" to the invitation to friendship as well as the possibility of a "yes." In his wisdom he has given an awesome role to the fundamental choices of the human person.

> God in the beginning created human beings
>   and made them subject to their own free choice.
> If you choose, you can keep the commandments;
>   loyalty is doing the will of God.
> Set before you are fire and water;
>   to whatever you choose, stretch out your hand.
> Before everyone are life and death,
>   whichever they choose will be given them.
> (Sir 15:14–17, NAB)

A Strong Delusion?

As regards God sending upon them a strong delusion to make them believe what is false, light is shed on this by noting what is taught in Romans 1.

> For the wrath of God is revealed from heaven against all ungodliness and wickedness of men who by their wickedness suppress the truth. For what can be known about God is plain to them, because God has shown it to them. Ever since the creation of the world his invisible nature, namely, his eternal power and deity, has been clearly perceived in the things that have been made. So they are without excuse; for although they knew God they did not honor him as God or give thanks to him, but they became futile in their thinking and their senseless minds were darkened. Claiming to be wise, they became fools, and exchanged the glory of the immortal God for images resembling mortal man or birds or animals or reptiles.

Therefore God gave them up in the lusts of their hearts to impurity, to the dishonoring of their bodies among themselves, because they exchanged the truth about God for a lie and worshiped and served the creature rather than the Creator, who is blessed forever! Amen. For this reason God gave them up to dishonorable passions. Their women exchanged natural relations for unnatural, and the men likewise gave up natural relations with women and were consumed with passion for one another, men committing shameless acts with men and receiving in their own persons the due penalty for their error. And since they did not see fit to acknowledge God, God gave them up to a base mind and to improper conduct. They were filled with all manner of wickedness, evil, covetousness, malice. Full of envy, murder, strife, deceit, malignity, they are gossips, slanderers, haters of God, insolent, haughty, boastful, inventors of evil, disobedient to parents, foolish, faithless, heartless, ruthless. Though they know God's decree that those who do such things deserve to die, they not only do them but approve those who practice them. (Rom 1:18–32)

God wills that those who reject his revelation of himself, whether it is in nature or the Gospel, be permitted to live the consequences of their rejection. The consequences of not honoring God or giving him thanks is that we become foolish in our thinking, our minds become darkened, and we think we are so smart and enlightened but become absolutely stupid, blind, and dark. The strong delusion that God "sends" is his decision to honor the choice of human freedom and to allow the consequences of unbelief and disobedience to play out as it were. Not only are our minds plunged into delusion, but there is now no longer the light to guide our actions, and we are at the mercy of our disordered desires; weakened by original and actual sin, all too ready to embrace the "wisdom" of our culture, we plunge into perverse sexuality and all manner of evil.

These texts provide an amazing insight into what we see happening in the collapse of our culture and the plunge of our nations into a new paganism with all its superstitions, deceptions, and barbaric practices.

Vexed Souls

The pain and anguish among God's people is growing. How often do I hear from godly mothers and fathers, grandmothers and grandfathers, who are in anguish as their children and grandchildren, some who went to Catholic schools, lost their faith through corrupt teaching, or have been engulfed in the powerful "peer pressure" of the intellectual elites of our culture who almost as a badge of belonging have to trumpet that they are "post Christian." It reminds me of some remarkable words of our first pope, Peter.

> But false prophets also arose among the people, just as there will be false teachers among you, who will secretly bring in destructive heresies, even denying the Master who bought them, bringing upon themselves swift destruction. And many will follow their licentiousness, and because of them the way of truth will be reviled. And in their greed they will exploit you with false words; from of old their condemnation has not been idle, and their destruction has not been asleep. For if the Lord rescued righteous Lot, greatly distressed by the licentiousness of the wicked (for by what that righteous man saw and heard as he lived among them, he was vexed in his righteous soul day after day with their lawless deeds), then the Lord knows how to rescue the godly from trial, and to keep the unrighteous under punishment until the day of judgment, and especially those who indulge in the lust of defiling passion and despise authority. (2 Pet 2:1–22)

What did Lot see and hear that vexed his righteous soul day after day? We find out what this is by looking at Genesis, chapters 18 and 19.

Abraham has failed in his plea to spare the corrupt city of Sodom and so two angels, in the appearance of men, go to the city to rescue Abrahams's nephew Lot and family. As nightfall comes, Lot's house is surrounded by the young and old males in the city who demand that the two guests be turned over to them for the purposes of homosexual abuse. Lot is horrified and goes outside to beg them not to do such a deed, even offering his virgin daughters to them, but they "press hard" against him and threaten to do even worse to him as they try to break down the door. At that point the angels reach out and pull Lot inside the house and blind the mob so that they can't carry out their abomination. The next day Sodom, along with Gomorrah, is destroyed.

The pressure in our own day to not only tolerate homosexuality but to approve it and consider it morally acceptable is becoming so great that those who resist are called bigots; those who believe God's word that those who do such things will not inherit the kingdom of God and are brave enough to say so are charged with hate speech! Passing on what the Church has taught for two thousand years about the eternal consequences of persisting in serious sexual sin is vilified as "lacking compassion." Yet precisely out of his profound compassion God reveals to us the ways that lead to life and death. We neglect them at our eternal peril. And not to tell the truth to those we love is to be guilty of a genuine lack of compassion.

These are hard words to hear! Many of us, perhaps all of us, have people we love dearly — family members, relatives, friends, neighbors, fellow parishioners — that have been ensnared in the lies of the evil one. And they are doing deeds or are approving them in others, which Scripture makes clear will exclude us from the Kingdom of God. What to do? With love in our hearts and tears in our eyes we need to keep on praying for their salvation, keep on assuring them of our love. But we must not agree that what they are doing or approving in others is anything other than a sad deception. It will lead to unhappiness in this life and eternal separation from God if not repented from before death.

But preaching the truth isn't easy!

> And the word of the Lord spread throughout all the region. But the Jews incited the devout women of high standing and the leading men of the city, and stirred up persecution against Paul and Barnabas and drove them out of their district. But they shook off the dust from their feet against them and went to Iconium. And the disciples were filled with joy and with the Holy Spirit. (Acts 13:49–52)

As Christian culture collapses and we again face a situation that has more in common with the early Church than anything we've known in our lifetime, the words of the early Church become more and more meaningful and applicable.

It's clear that the faith that saves is not just a one-time assent but an assent that leads to a life of fidelity to Christ and his teachings.

> "Truly, truly I say to you, the hour is coming, and now is, when the dead will hear the voice of the Son of God, and those who hear will live. For as the Father has life in himself, so he has granted the Son also to have life in himself, and has given him authority to execute judgment, because he is the Son of man. Do not marvel at this; for the hour is coming when all who are in the tombs will hear his voice and come forth, those who have done good, to the resurrection of life, and those who have done evil, to the resurrection of judgment." (Jn 5:25–29)

As the Apostle Paul put it:

> For the grace of God has appeared for the salvation of all men, training us to renounce irreligion and worldly passions, and to live sober, upright, and godly lives in this

world, awaiting our blessed hope, the appearing of the glory of our great God and Savior Jesus Christ, who gave himself for us to redeem us from all iniquity and to purify for himself a people of his own who are zealous for good deeds. Declare these things; exhort and reprove with all authority. (Tit 2:11–15)

The apostles faithfully passed on the very teaching of Jesus about the urgency of response in light of the coming judgment. Faith is necessary but so is repentance. It's not those who simply say "Lord, Lord" who will enter the Kingdom but those who obey the word of the Lord.

The times of ignorance God overlooked, but now he commands men everywhere to repent, because he has fixed a day on which he will judge the world in righteousness by a man whom he has appointed, and of this he has given assurance to all men by raising him from the dead. (Acts 17:30–31)

"How Can You Believe in a God That Would Condemn People to Hell for All Eternity?"

It might be well here to offer a few thoughts on the judgment to condemnation — hell. There's a great contemporary effort to make clear that God condemns no one to hell but people choose this for themselves, and there is a profound truth to this view. While there is a profound truth to this view of things, it is also greatly motivated by the worthy desire to take away an obstacle to belief for those who say: "How can you believe in a God that sends people to hell for all eternity?"

Indeed there are words of Jesus that explicitly communicate this truth:

"If anyone hears my sayings and does not keep them, I do not judge him; for I did not come to judge the world but to save the world. He who rejects me and does not receive my sayings has a judge; the word that I have spoken will be his judge on the last day. For I have not spoken on my own authority; the Father who sent me has himself given me commandment what to say and what to speak. And I know that his commandment is eternal life. What I say, therefore, I say as the Father has bidden me." (Jn 12:47–50)

On the other hand we run the risk of obscuring the transcendent holiness and justice of God by conforming him to our limited creaturely conceptions of justice. God has established the order of the universe. By his just decree those who reject the sacrifice of Christ and are disobedient to his salvific words will be condemned. Truly, as far above the earth as is the sky so are God's thoughts above our thoughts. We make a huge mistake in "cutting God down to size" by not realizing that our human standards of justice are completely inadequate for articulating the transcendent holiness and justice of God. We diminish his Lordship by not recognizing that while people may condemn themselves to hell, God has established this order with its consequences as the passage from Acts 17:30–31 makes clear. The judgment of all mankind comes from the Father through Christ. And there are many other texts that make this clear as well.

Repentance means changing our mind and changing how we live to bring our whole beings into harmony with God's will for human life. Repentance isn't something at root "negative" but profoundly positive. Scripture calls it "life-giving repentance" (Acts 11:18). Jesus himself preached repentance as a fundamental aspect of his message and commanded the disciples to do the same.

"Now after John was arrested, Jesus came into Galilee, preaching the gospel of God, and saying, 'The time is fulfilled, and the kingdom of God is at hand; repent, and believe in the gospel'" (Mk 1:14–15).

In the resurrection encounter with the disciples in Jerusalem, recounted by Luke, Jesus tells them what they are to preach.

> "Thus it is written, that the Christ should suffer and on the third day rise from the dead, and that repentance and forgiveness of sins should be preached in his name to all nations, beginning from Jerusalem." (Lk 24:46–48)

And repentance for the forgiveness of sins was what the apostles preached. When the sensational healing of the crippled man whom everyone knew happened, Peter explained that was a sign given by God to draw people to the source of that healing, Jesus himself, and the necessity of faith in that Name, along with repentance and the forgiveness of sins.

> "And now brethren, I know that you acted in ignorance, as did also your rulers. But what God foretold by the mouth of all the prophets, that his Christ should suffer, he thus fulfilled. Repent therefore, and turn again, that your sins may be blotted out, that times of refreshing may come from the presence of the Lord, and that he may send the Christ appointed for you, Jesus, whom heaven must receive until the time for establishing all that God spoke by the mouth of his holy prophets from of old. Moses said, "The Lord God will raise up for you a prophet from your brethren as he raised me up. You shall listen to him in whatever he tells you. And it shall be that every soul that does not listen to that prophet shall be destroyed from the people.... God, having raised up his servant, sent him to you first, to bless you in turning every one of you from your wickedness." (Acts 3:17–26)

And what was the response? "Many believed" but not all. They were arrested by the leaders (Acts 4:1–4).

The letter to the Hebrews teaches that "he became the source of salvation to all who obey him" (Heb 5:9), echoing the teaching of Jesus that not everyone who says "Lord, Lord" will enter the kingdom but those who actually do the will of the Father (Mt 7:21–23).

Repentance must involve a change of life, bringing our lives into harmony with God's will for human life. This means turning away from sin and yielding to the transforming work of the Spirit so that we may grow in virtue. Unfortunately there are many today who, deceived, believe that it is possible to claim God's mercy but still live a life of sin. This deception was already prevalent in the early Church. Jesus had warned about it. The Apostles taught against it.

> Do you not know that the unrighteous will not inherit the kingdom of God? Do not be deceived, neither the immoral, nor idolaters, nor adulterers, nor homosexuals, nor thieves, nor the greedy nor drunkards, nor revilers, nor robbers will inherit the kingdom of God. (1 Cor 6:9–10 [*Note:* The Greek word translated as homosexuals refers to the active practice of homosexuality, not a simple inclination.])

As Paul often does, he repeats what is particularly important for us to know:

> For you were called to freedom, brethren: only do not use your freedom as an opportunity for the flesh, but through love be servants of one another.... Now the works of the flesh are plain: immorality, impurity, licentiousness, idolatry, sorcery, enmity, strife, jealousy, anger, selfishness, dissension, party spirit, envy, drunkenness, carousing, and the like. I warn you, as I warned you before, that those who do such things shall not inherit the kingdom of God. (Gal 5:13, 19–21)

We also find this clear warning in Ephesians:

> Be sure of this, that no immoral or impure man, or one who is covetous (that is, an idolater), has any inheritance in the kingdom of Christ and of God. Let no one deceive you with empty words, for it is because of these things that

the wrath of God comes upon the sons of disobedience. (Eph 5:5–6)

Faith in Christ and repentance from sin are essential parts of the message we have been called to proclaim. We are not at liberty to add to or subtract from the word we have been entrusted with. And today we have to be explicit about which sins will exclude us from the kingdom since there has been such a silence on sin, and such deceptions widely promulgated.

The apostles were clearly conscious of having been entrusted with the clear content of the message they were to proclaim. Paul described his awesome encounter with the risen Lord on his way to persecute Christians in Damascus. He tells us what the Lord communicated to him in that encounter. He was to proclaim to those whom the Lord was sending him: "to open their eyes, that they may turn from darkness to light and from the power of Satan to God, that they may receive forgiveness of sins and a place among those who are sanctified by faith in me" (Acts 26:17–18).

Jesus commanded the apostles to preach this message and they did.

On the day of Pentecost the people were cut to the heart by Peter's preaching and, receiving the word preached, in faith, asked what they should do in response. Peter told them: "'Repent, and be baptized every one of you in the name of Jesus Christ for the forgiveness of your sins; and you shall receive the gift of the Holy Spirit.'... And he testified with many other words and exhorted them, saying, 'Save yourselves from this crooked generation'" (Acts 2:37–40).

The Necessity of Baptism

Since this book is focused on the "new evangelization," which by definition concerns the "re-evangelization" of people who are for the most part already baptized, we will not elaborate on the necessity of baptism other than to declare firmly that if someone is not baptized Jesus requires that they be baptized in order to enter the kingdom. This is the teaching of Jesus, the teaching and practice of the Apostles, and the teaching of the *Catechism of the Catholic Church* (see CCC 1257–1260). Faith and repentance that leads to baptism is the only way the Church knows for sure that people attain salvation.

Embracing the Command to Preach the Gospel Today

And this of course needs to be our message also. Not to tell people the truth about what we must do to be saved is to do them an almost unforgivable disservice. Not to tell people the truth about the way that leads to eternal life and the way that leads to eternal death is to mislead them, and we will be held accountable.

The Lord told Ezekiel that he must speak the truth to people about repentance and sin, and if people heeded what he said, they would be saved. But, the Lord told Ezekiel, if he neglected to tell them the truth, he would be held responsible for their destruction.

Paul was also very aware of his responsibility to tell his hearers the whole truth about salvation.

> Therefore I testify to you this day that I am innocent of the blood of all of you, for I did not shrink from declaring to you the whole counsel of God. (Acts 20:26–27)

Resistance to the Gospel Is to Be Expected

Rightfully, we want to find ways of presenting the Gospel in the most attractive light possible to maximize the chances of positive responses. But, if we are going to present the whole truth — as we must — which includes the necessity of responding in faith and repentance and baptism (if not already baptized) — we can expect that some will reject the message with varying degrees of mockery and hostility, either temporarily or even permanently. We must in our sharing of the Gospel at some point explain clearly that what is at stake is eternal life or death, heaven or hell, and that there are serious consequences that flow from the rejection of the gift of God's only Son.

We need only to look at how the best preaching of the Gospel that has ever happened in the history of the world — that of Jesus himself and the Apostles — was often rejected to prepare ourselves to walk the same path that they walked.

The Apostles, when they were met with rejection, recalled the words of Psalm 107:

> After their release they went back to their own people and reported what the chief priests and elders had told them. And when they heard it, they raised their voices to God with one accord and said, "Sovereign Lord, maker of heaven and earth and the sea and all that is in them, you said by the holy Spirit through the mouth of our father David, your servant:
>
> 'Why did the Gentiles rage
>   and the peoples entertain folly?
> The kings of the earth took their stand
>   and the princes gathered together
>   against the Lord and against his anointed.'"
>
> (Acts 4:23–26)

The Apostles knew that this opposition was being permitted by God and that they needed to proceed with preaching the Gospel in the face of the opposition depending on the power of God to sustain them.

After being strictly ordered to stop proclaiming Jesus, the Apostles were arrested again after continuing to preach.

But Peter and the apostles answered, "We must obey God rather than men. The God of our fathers raised Jesus whom you killed by hanging him on a tree. God exalted him at his right hand as Leader and Savior to give repentance to Israel and forgiveness of sins. And we are witnesses to these things, and so is the Holy Spirit whom God has given to those who obey him." (Acts 5:29–32)

Notice that repentance and forgiveness of sins is being offered as a gift, through Jesus, but gifts need to be accepted. Were there conversions as a result of this proclamation? Not this time.

"When they heard this they were enraged and wanted to kill them" (Acts 5:33).

Gamaliel, a respected leader, prevailed upon them not to take such drastic measures but to see how things played out.

"So they took his advice, and when they had called in the apostles, they beat them and charged them not to speak in the name of Jesus, and let them go" (Acts 5:40).

The apostles' response?

"Then they left the presence of the council, rejoicing that they were counted worthy to suffer dishonor for the name. And every day in the temple and at home they did not cease teaching and preaching Jesus as the Christ" (Acts 5:41–42).

Can We Really Say These Things to People and Have Them Listen?

I admit it. What is revealed in Scripture is shocking to contemporary ears! So, how can it be shared in the most effective way?

Those of us who have teaching and preaching responsibility absolutely have to find ways to communicate these truths clearly whether it is in homilies, or religious education classes, or sacramental preparation or RCIA. We are commanded to do so. It is not an option.

At the same time we have to be "led by the Spirit" as to the time, the place, and the manner in which these truths should be shared. For those who teach and preach based on the Lectionary or the *Catechism of the Catholic Church* these difficult topics will be brought up in the cycle of readings and in the elements of the *Catechism*. We should not shy away from them or skip over them or downplay them but "tell it like it is." We should emphasize that these things are revealed to us by Jesus and the Apostles and taught clearly to this day by the Church, because of God's great love for us. The Lord wants us to be saved rather than lost!

That familiar text of John 3:16 provides a good model for us. The whole plan of God is all about love. That love comes to us in the most amazing way, in the person of God's beloved Son. Great feats of heroism aren't required by way of response but simply faith, a faith that leads to repentance, conversion, and obedience. The reward for responding to God's offer of love in the person of Jesus is nothing less than eternal life! The consequence of rejecting God's love in the gift of Jesus is nothing less than to perish, eternally separated from God by our own choice. This gives a good model of the relative "proportion" of attention and time that should be given to the different elements of the message.

When the inevitable questions are raised — as they will be — we should be prepared to give answers, some of which I have attempted to offer in this short book.[59]

Those of us who aren't involved in preaching and teaching in a formal way will have opportunities arise in the course of our normal interaction with family and friends to communicate the truth about salvation.

We must remember that the eternal destinies of everyone we love or may encounter are hanging in the balance. The witness of our lives and the wisdom and truth of our words may make an eternal difference for people.

The four elements of Catholic lay mission as described in the *Decree on the Apostolate of Lay People* from Vatican II, which we have referenced in chapter III, provide a good framework for understanding our mission. Let's review them.

All mission must be rooted in living the life that we are encouraging others to live, and so the witness/example of our own life is the necessary foundation for all lay evangelization.

A second important element is the works of mercy. Serving people who simply need help whether there is an opportunity to witness to our faith in words, or not.

A third element is "renewing the temporal order," which includes being a responsible citizen and participating as we are able in making the world a better place to live in. We do this not just through works of personal or organized charity, but through contributing to the betterment of the structures in which human life must take place. This means taking a concern for educational opportunity, health care, the environment, action in favor of peace and justice, and defending human life from conception to natural death.

But as Vatican II points out, the core of evangelization includes a necessary fourth element: speaking about Jesus in words as well as in the example of our life, with a view toward helping people to come to faith who don't have faith, or helping people grow in faith into true disciples of the Lord, and evangelists themselves.

One of the most effective ways of sharing our faith is to give some thought to how best to speak about how we came to a committed relationship with the Lord in a way that would be most understandable depending on whom we're talking to. As I mentioned in chapter III, in all my classes at the seminary I have the seminarians, priests, and laypeople prepare a five-minute testimony that is geared toward unbelievers or fallen away Catholics.

Another good way of sharing our faith is to invite someone to go with us to hear a talk or attend a retreat or day of renewal or reflection that could awaken faith in them.

Another good way is to offer someone a book or CD or DVD that we've read or listened to or watched that could awaken faith.

At the same time we have to be aware that we're not just offering to people an "enrichment" for their life or an "optional extra" for "spiritually inclined people." We're "fishing for men," trying to lead people into a saving relationship with Christ, or back to a saving relationship with Christ, through faith and repentance. We don't necessarily have to "lead" with repentance, but at some point, if serious sin is involved, repentance is a must. It really is heaven or hell that is at stake, and at some point that needs to be shared.

Underlying all our efforts at evangelization is persevering intercessory prayer for those who may be on the wide path leading to destruction. Where there is life there is hope, and so we must never tire of praying for someone's conversion even if for many years — or never — we don't see positive signs of conversion. As the Scripture says, the prayer of a righteous person is powerful in its effect (Jas 5:16). The Lord may also lead us to fast for someone's salvation for a certain time or in a certain way. And occasionally he may even lead us to a life-long intercessory fast in anyone of a number of small ways.

When we are sharing these wonderful and challenging truths with people, we must make it clear that we're not judging them. "No, I'm not saying that you're going to hell. What I'm saying is that you should really pay attention to what Jesus says about what will lead us to hell if we don't repent and turn to him for forgiveness and new life." In my own efforts, I try to make clear that, because I love someone, I want them to hear what God has revealed to us about how to end up eternally happy and how to avoid the tragic failure of our life if we die unrepentant and unfaithful.

I've had to endure my share of "I don't want to talk about that. I don't want to hear about that." And I've had to back off from words and be content with prayer and love but from time to time. I, and I think all of us, need to raise the issue again even if we're cut off again. We must never give the people we are evangelizing the impression or outright agreement with them that it's alright to commit those sins that Jesus says will exclude us from the Kingdom. It's challenging to "love the sinner" and not the sin, but we have to do it, even if it means having to hear "if you really loved me, you would accept me — and what I'm doing — as I am." Our unconditional love can never mean doing the one we love the profound disservice of encouraging them in their sin, as painful as it may be. That would be like a doctor telling a patient that has cancer that "they'll be alright" and not tell them the treatment that would actually save their life. Gross malpractice. Profoundly misguided compassion.

This doesn't mean we have to take the "bull in a china shop" approach to sharing the truth, but it does mean at some point we have to share it. Speaking the truth in love, possibly with tears in our eyes and grief in our heart, for those whom we love who are perishing, needs to be done, or we will be held responsible.

> For many, of whom I have often told you and now tell you even with tears, walk as enemies of the cross of Christ. Their end is destruction, their god is the belly, and they glory in their shame, with minds set on earthly things. But our commonwealth is in heaven, and from it we await a Savior, the Lord Jesus Christ, who will change our lowly body to be like his glorious body, by the power which enables him even to subject all things to himself. (Phil 3:18–21)

This also doesn't mean that if we are rejected and the message rejected that we have done anything wrong. Jesus and the apostles were often rejected, but they knew even so the Word had to be spoken; people had to be given a chance, even if they ignored it or it made them angry.

Whether it be by sharing our testimony, passing on a book, inviting them to an event where the Gospel will be preached — always supported by intercessory prayer and perhaps fasting — we have been given the truly awesome privilege and responsibility of participating in the Lord's ongoing mission to seek and to save those who are lost. What great joy there is in heaven when just one sinner repents!

About the Author

Ralph Martin holds a doctorate in sacred theology (S.T.D.) from the Pontifical University of St. Thomas (the Angelicum) in Rome. He serves as the Director of Graduate Theology Programs in the New Evangelization at Sacred Heart Major Seminary in the Archdiocese of Detroit (www.shms.edu). He is also the founder and president of Renewal Ministries, a Catholic ministry devoted to renewal and evangelization (www.renewalministries.net). He is the host of the long-running EWTN television and radio program *The Choices We Face*. A well-known author, his most recent books are *The Fulfillment of All Desire: A Guidebook for the Journey to God Based on the Wisdom of the Saints*, and *Will Many Be Saved? What Vatican II Actually Teaches and Its Implications for the New Evangelization*. He and his wife, Anne, live in Ann Arbor, Michigan, and are parents of six and grandparents of thirteen. He was appointed by Pope Benedict XVI as a Consultor to the Pontifical Council for the New Evangelization.

Appendix

Biblical Orientations for the New Evangelization

MARY HEALY AND PETER WILLIAMSON

Abstract: As the Church embarks on a new evangelization it is essential to reflect on the biblical paradigm of the Church's evangelizing mission. This article first draws on the Gospels and the Acts of the Apostles to shed light on the task, message, and goal of evangelization. The task includes Jesus' imperative to wait for divine empowerment and then to go where the unevangelized can be found. The message (*kerygma*) is the good news of salvation in Jesus Christ, which should be distinguished from other aspects of the Church's teaching and pastoral mission. The goal is to form not merely converts but disciples who "observe all that [Jesus has] commanded...." (Mt 28:20). The article then examines Paul's mission as depicted in Acts and the Epistles to learn from the Apostle's reliance on the Holy Spirit to persuade his hearers (1 Cor 2:5) and his missionary methods, which include establishing communities, collaborating with coworkers, mentoring younger leaders, and prioritizing the reading and interpreting of Scripture.

What does Scripture itself teach and model regarding evangelization? This question merits careful attention as the universal Church pursues the call to a new evangelization.[60] In his apostolic exhortation *Verbum Domini* Pope Benedict XVI calls for Catholic theology, preaching, catechesis, spirituality, and pastoral outreach to become more biblical, while simultaneously calling for Catholic biblical scholarship to become more ecclesial. He urges pastors and the faithful alike to make the Bible "the inspiration of every ordinary and extraordinary pastoral outreach" and "to recognize the importance of this emphasis on the Bible."[61] He repeatedly insists on the necessity of direct contact with the biblical texts themselves and of greater familiarity with the content of Scripture on the part of all Catholics.

This insistence recalls an important but neglected statement of Vatican Council II: "All the preaching of the Church, like *the Christian religion itself, must be nourished and regulated* by Sacred Scripture."[62] Because Scripture, as inspired by God, "contains the divine word (cf. 2 Tim 3:16) in an altogether singular way,"[63] it has a uniquely normative role in Christian life. It also has a unique power to touch and change the human heart, as *Verbum Domini* frequently stresses.[64] Its authority is distinct from and more foundational than that of ecclesial documents, which are in essence authoritative interpretations of Scripture in light of Tradition.[65] The unique status of Scripture suggests that in every endeavor the Church should *begin* with Scripture and remain rooted in it, rather than first formulating plans and then searching for suitable biblical texts to adorn them, as we are often tempted to do.[66]

This article will explore the implications for evangelization of Pope Benedict XVI's call for a return to Scripture by considering what the New Testament teaches and models regarding the proclamation of the gospel. As Pope Paul VI stated in his apostolic letter on evangelization, "The whole of the New Testament, and in a special way the Acts of the Apostles, bears witness to a privileged and in a sense exemplary moment of this missionary effort that will subsequently leave its mark on the whole history of the

Church."[67] The New Testament writings are not only a source of theological doctrine or of historical data about early Christianity, but also a blueprint for the life and mission of the Church today. The apostolic church contains the DNA, so to speak, for the church in every age. Although the church learns from other great missionaries and evangelists in her tradition — such as Patrick, Boniface, Cyril and Methodius, Francis and Dominic, Francis Xavier and Matteo Ricci, Frances Xavier Cabrini, and Katherine Drexel — all these looked in turn to the preaching of Jesus, the Acts of the Apostles, and the writings of Paul as the paradigm for their missionary endeavors. Of course this does not mean rigid duplication of biblical patterns. Within the New Testament itself there is considerable flexibility of method as well as adaptation of the message for diverse audiences.[68]

This article is intended as a work of biblical theology directed to the situation of the Church today, a kind of pastoral actualization. We will consider what the New Testament reveals about the task, message, goal, means, and methods of evangelization and reflect on its relevance to the present situation. Space permits only an overview, touching on many points that merit more extensive biblical analysis and pastoral reflection.[69]

1. The Task of Evangelization

The church's task of evangelization, as Luke-Acts presents it, is commissioned by Jesus in a directive with two distinct elements: the command to "wait" and the command to "go." We will consider each of these in turn.

Awaiting divine empowerment

In Luke's version of the great commission, given at the end of his gospel and again at the beginning of Acts, there is a strong emphasis on the fact that the apostles' mission does not begin immediately. After assigning the apostles the momentous task of being his witnesses "to all nations" (Lk 24:47–48), Jesus' first instruction is to wait: "Stay in the city until you are clothed with power from on high" (Lk 24:49). "He charged them not to depart from Jerusalem, but to wait for the promise of the Father," namely, that they would be "baptized with the Holy Spirit" (Acts 1:4–5).[70] Paradoxically, the first imperative of the Christian mission is to *wait* for empowerment from on high.

The promise of divine empowerment is fulfilled at Pentecost when the disciples are "filled with the Holy Spirit" (Acts 2:4) with the immediate consequence that they begin to "speak ... the mighty works of God," that is, to evangelize, Jews representing the nations of the known world (Acts 2:5–11). They are overflowing with joy and are now able to proclaim the good news with clarity, boldness, and conviction. The Pentecostal outpouring of the Holy Spirit is, as Luke presents it, the absolute prerequisite for carrying out the church's daunting mission.

Luke expects that some of his readers will catch the irony in the accusation of the bystanders at Pentecost, "They are filled with new wine (*gleukos*)" (Acts 2:13). In the prophetic literature, new wine (or sweet wine) is an image of the abundance of life promised by God in the messianic age. "Behold, the days are coming, says the LORD, when ... the mountains shall drip sweet wine (*glukasmon*), and all the hills shall flow with it" (Amos 9:13 LXX; cf. Joel 3:18). In the Synoptic Gospels Jesus indicates that he came to bring new wine, which must be put into fresh wineskins (Lk 5:37–38). Read in light of Acts, the new wine is the Spirit; the fresh wineskins are transformed human hearts.

This experience of the "sweet wine" of divine life is what imbues the disciples with compelling dynamism to proclaim the good news of salvation in Christ.[71] Like Jeremiah, who felt the word of God as a fire burning in his bones (Jer 20:9), they cannot keep the word of God to themselves. The transformation wrought by the Spirit is particularly evident in Peter. The Peter who had found the idea of a suffering Messiah incomprehensible and had denied his Lord (Lk 9:45; 22:56–61) now recognizes the paschal mystery as the fulfillment of God's gracious plan of salvation (Acts 2:14–36) and confidently proclaims this good news to a crowd of thousands. He heals a cripple with a word, boldly defies the Sanhedrin, and endures beating and imprisonment joyfully. Peter's conduct exemplifies the fact that the church is now characterized by the divine "power" Jesus had promised (Lk 24:48; Acts 1:8).[72]

Following the descent of the Spirit, Luke reports an explosion of missionary activity and the consequent prodigious growth of the church. Throughout the remainder of Acts the Holy Spirit is the initiator, guide, and dynamic force that propels the church's mission. Although Pentecost is a unique, once-for-all event, renewed outpourings of the Spirit occur on numerous occasions and are continually interwoven with the story (8:14–17; 10:44–46; 19:6). Even the Jerusalem church needs a new filling with the Spirit to face new challenges (Acts 4:31).

We would do well to consider whether the church today has sufficiently taken into account this link between Pentecost and evangelization. Although all acknowledge that "the Holy Spirit is the principal agent of evangelization,"[73] it is common to presume that since the first Pentecost the Church enjoys the fullness of the Spirit, and can get on with the job of proclaiming the gospel. But a fresh outpouring of power from on high is as necessary today as it was in the early church. To take the New Testament witness seriously is to conclude that *there can be no new evangelization without a new Pentecost.*

In his visit to the United States, Pope Benedict XVI gave voice to this insight when in St. Patrick's Cathedral he said, "Let us implore from God the grace of a new Pentecost for the church in America. May tongues of fire, combining burning love of God and neighbor with zeal for the spread of Christ's kingdom, descend on all present!" Although there are many indications that such a new Pentecost has begun,[74] the grace of the Spirit cannot be presumed, but must be continuously sought in faith (Lk 11:9–13). The command for Christ's disciples to "stay in the city until you are clothed with power from on high" needs to be relived in every generation. Otherwise we risk attempting to carry out a divine task with human resources.

Going to the lost

The three Synoptic versions of the great commission are equally emphatic that the task of evangelization consists in a dynamic outward movement that has no geographical limits. Jesus commands his disciples, "Go into all the world and preach the gospel to all creation" (Mk 16:15); "Go make disciples of all nations" (Mt 28:20). In Acts, the mission is to be carried out in increasingly widening circles: "you shall be my witnesses in Jerusalem and in all Judea and Samaria and to the end of the earth" (Acts 1:8). Jesus' instruction is not to sit and wait for seekers to knock at the church's door, but to go to where the unevangelized can be found, as he himself did in the Gospels.[75] Thus the second imperative of the New Evangelization is to *go*.

Other biblical texts such as the parables of the lost sheep, lost coin, and lost sons (Lk 15) and the command to "go out to the highways and hedges" to invite guests to the banquet (Lk 14:23) add a further dimension to this truth. They suggest that God has a preferential option for the lost. "Jesus Christ came into the world to save sinners" (1 Tim 1:15), "to seek and to save the lost" (Lk 19:10; see Lk 5:31–32; Rom 5:6–8; Eph 2:4–5). Lost sinners must, therefore, be the priority of Jesus' disciples as well.

While not all are called to foreign missions, all are called to go beyond the sheepfold where the 99 may be found to look for the lost.[76] However, it must be acknowledged that after twenty centuries of Christianity, the culture and habits of the Church today are largely directed toward maintenance rather than mission, toward ministering to those inside the church rather than seeking those outside it.[77] As Raniero Cantalamessa points out, "We are more prepared by our past to be 'shepherds' than to be 'fishers' of men; that is, better prepared to nourish people that come to the Church then to bring new people to the Church, or to catch again those who have fallen away and live outside of her."[78] By far most of the formation given to future priests and pastoral ministers focuses on those who already practice their faith. To succeed at the New Evangelization, the church must reorient her culture, institutions, and formation toward proclamation and mission. Both clergy and laity must reject an attitude of passivity and take an active responsibility for going out and making disciples.

Jesus' use of the word "lost" (*apolōlos*, literally "perished, destroyed") for those who have not yet repented (Lk 19:10) also points to a recognition that nothing less than the eternal salvation or loss of human beings is at stake in the proclamation of the gospel.[79] In the version of the great commission found in the longer ending of Mark, Jesus warns, "Whoever believes and is baptized will be saved, but whoever does not believe will be condemned" (Mk 16:16). The idea of two ways, two ultimate destinations for human existence, is one of the most consistent themes of the New Testament: there are the weeds and the wheat (Mt 13:30), the sheep and the goats (Mt 25:31:35), the foolish and the wise (Mt 7:24–27; 25:1–12), the branches that bear fruit and those that are cut off and thrown in the fire (Jn 15:1–6), the wide gate that leads to destruction and the narrow gate that leads to life (Mt 7:13–14), those who hear the word and those who ignore it (Mk 4:13–20), those who come to the light and those who love the darkness (Jn 3:19–21), those who receive Jesus and those who do not (Jn 1:11–12), the repentant believing thief and the mocking unbelieving thief (Lk 23:39–32).

A presumption of universal salvation that is not grounded in Scripture has seeped into some theology and the mentality of many Catholics.[80] Sometimes this is due to a misunderstanding of *Lumen Gentium* 16, which affirms the possibility of eternal salvation for "those who, through no fault of their own, do not know the Gospel of Christ or his Church, but who nevertheless seek God with a sincere heart, and moved by grace, try ... to do his will as they know it through the dictates of their conscience." While this teaching offers an important corrective to the idea that those who do not know Christ are *ipso facto* condemned, *Lumen Gentium* 16 goes on to make clear that the outcome is not always positive:

> But very often, deceived by the Evil One, people have lost their way in their thinking, have exchanged the truth of God for a lie and served the creature rather than the Creator (see Rom 1:21 and 25). Or else, living and dying in this world without God, they are exposed to ultimate despair.

Biblical texts such as Rom 5:18; 1 Tim 2:4; Titus 2:11; 2 Pet 3:9 are sometimes used as proof texts to support the idea that all will be saved. However, an examination of these texts in their literary contexts and in the context of all the New Testament writings demonstrates that the authors consider salvation to depend on faith, baptism, and repentance manifest in changed conduct (Lk 3:8; Jn 3:18–20; 1 Cor 6:9–11). The authors give no indication that they expect that everyone will make that response. After preaching in Pisidian Antioch, Paul and Barnabas tell those who reject their message that by rejecting the gospel, "you … judge yourselves unworthy of eternal life" (Acts 13:46). Two verses later Luke summarizes the outcome of Paul's preaching in that city: "as many as were appointed to eternal life believed" (Acts 13:48).

Scripture thus presents the preaching of the gospel and people's response to it as having the greatest consequences imaginable, a fact that inspired the zeal of St. Paul and of missionaries throughout the history of the Church (cf. 1 Cor 9:22; 2 Cor 5:10–15). Conversely, when the necessity of proclaiming and accepting the gospel is obscured, zeal for evangelization recedes.

2. The Message of Evangelization

Recent ecclesial documents, including the *Instrumentum laboris* for the 2012 Synod, have tended to speak of two distinct senses of the term "evangelize."

In its precise sense, evangelization is the *missio ad gentes* directed to those who do not know Christ. In a wider sense, it is used to describe ordinary pastoral work.[81]

In the wider sense, evangelization comprises the entirety of Christian mission and pastoral care, including the proclamation of the gospel, catechesis, the sacraments, mystagogy, ongoing faith formation, and even the transformation of communities, institutions, the culture, and society as a whole. The New Testament, however, helps us recognize the importance of retaining the primary focus on evangelization in the strict sense, that is, *the announcement of the* kerygma, *the good news of salvation in Jesus Christ, with the goal of leading people to faith and conversion.* This is the meaning of *euangelizomai* in the New Testament.[82] As Pope Paul VI insisted,

> Evangelization will also always contain — as the foundation, center and … summit of its dynamism — a clear proclamation that, in Jesus Christ, the Son of God made man, who died and rose from the dead, salvation is offered to all men, as a gift of God's grace and mercy.[83]

This proclamation of the *kerygma*, however, is precisely the step that Catholics often tend to skip. When the primary focus on proclamation of the *kerygma* becomes obscured, the risk is that "evangelization" becomes a vague and diffuse term that means nothing more than "everything we're already doing," and new evangelization means "more of the same." The New Testament, in contrast, makes a clear distinction between the preaching of the *kerygma* and the teaching or catechesis that follows conversion (cf. Rom 15:20; 1 Cor 2:1–4; 3:6–10). As Fio Mascarenhas puts it,

> [T]he *kerygma* … had, so to speak, an explosive or germinating character; it was more like the seed that gives origin to the tree than the ripe fruit that is at the top of the tree. The *kerygma* was not obtained at all by summary, as if it

was the core of the tradition; but it was at the beginning of everything. From it all the rest was developed....[84]

The anointed preaching of the *kerygma* has an intrinsic power to awaken faith in the hearers. "So faith comes from hearing, and hearing through the word of Christ" (Rom 10:17). The church's joyful exclamation, "*Jesus is Lord!*" (cf. Rom 10:9; 2 Cor 4:5) has its own self-authenticating power; it makes present and operative that which it signifies. "Faith is born through the sudden and astonished recognition of the truth contained in the *kerygma*."[85]

For the New Evangelization to succeed, ministers of the word (and as much as possible, all the faithful) need to be able to proclaim the *kerygma* in a concise and convincing way. Surprisingly, this skill is often overlooked in ministerial formation. The Church's experience for many centuries has been that of catechizing members who were baptized as infants in social settings that fostered Christian faith. Today those environments have largely disappeared, and many baptized Catholics, like most non-Christians, have never heard the gospel proclaimed or made a deliberate choice to follow Christ as his disciple. As Pope John Paul II candidly observed, many Catholics have been baptized and catechized without ever having been *evangelized* — that is, without having heard the gospel in a way that led them to a personal encounter with Jesus Christ and a joyful surrender of their lives to him.[86] The absence of this step leads to what is by New Testament standards a sub-Christian life that is often unable to withstand the pressures of today's post-Christian culture.

What exactly is the gospel message that Christians are called to proclaim? The Protestant Reformation identified the gospel with the doctrine of justification by faith. Catholics often focus on *living* the gospel, that is, the ethical elements of Christ's teaching, especially the Sermon on the Mount and service to the poor and marginalized. Catholics also use "gospel" to refer to the whole of the Church's faith. All of these are valid uses of the term, but in the New Testament itself the meaning is more specific: it refers primarily to the gratuitous gift of salvation in Jesus Christ.[87]

The word *euangelion* occurs first on the lips of Jesus: "Jesus came into Galilee, proclaiming the gospel of God, and saying, 'The time is fulfilled, and the kingdom of God is at hand; repent and believe in the gospel'" (Mk 1:14–15). Matthew 4:23 summarizes Jesus' early ministry as "teaching in their synagogues and proclaiming the gospel of the kingdom and healing every disease ... among the people." Similarly, in Luke's account of Jesus' inaugural sermon at Nazareth, Jesus summarizes his mission as "to proclaim gospel to [literally, *evangelize*] the poor" (Lk 4:18). In Jesus' ministry, the essential content of the gospel is that in him, God has come to save his people and establish his victorious reign over the earth. Jesus' healings, exorcisms, and forgiveness of sins reveal God's decisive intervention in history, offering a foretaste of the future blessedness of the kingdom. They function as signs that disclose Jesus' identity and confirm the truth of his message. From the beginning, the gospel was not mere information but a proclamation in power that demanded a personal response of faith and repentance.

After Jesus' death and resurrection, and the fulfillment of his promise of the Holy Spirit (Acts 1:8; 2:33), the preaching of the gospel resumes. Now, however, its full content is revealed: it is the "good news about the kingdom of God and the name of Jesus Christ" (Acts 8:12; see 28:23, 31). The kingdom is fulfilled in the risen Jesus himself. What in Jesus' public ministry was "preaching the kingdom" becomes in the church's ministry "preaching the Lord Jesus" (Acts 11:20). Luke portrays seven sermons by Peter and Paul in Acts that make the content of the gospel message explicit.[88] They share a common core although they vary among themselves depending on the circumstances and on the audience the apostle is addressing.

It would be helpful if conferences of bishops, or those experienced in evangelization, could provide a summary of the *kerygma* drawn from Scripture, which evangelists today could learn and put to use. Such a summary might include elements like the following.[89]

> 1. God's infinite, unconditional, and personal love for every human being, and his desire that every person attain the fullness of life in communion with himself (Jn 3:16; 10:10; Eph 2:4–7).
>
> 2. The reason we do not experience this fullness of life: sin has separated us from God, introduced evil into the world, and left the human race in a desperate condition (Isa 59:2; Rom 3:23; Eph 2:1–3), ultimately leading to eternal death (Rom 5:12; 6:23).
>
> 3. The solution provided by God: God sent his Son Jesus to reveal the Father's love, to forgive our sins and reconcile us with God through his death and resurrection (Jn 15:9; Rom 5:8–10) and to fill us with his Holy Spirit (Acts 2:38; Rom 5:5).
>
> 4. Our part: to receive the gift of God by repenting from sin, believing in Jesus, and being baptized into the communion of his body, the Church (Mk 16:16; Jn 3:5–6; Rev 3:20).
>
> 5. Jesus' coming in glory as judge, at which time the dead will be raised and all will receive the just recompense for their deeds and their acceptance or refusal of God's grace, either eternal life or eternal separation from God (Jn 5:28–30; Acts 17:31; 2 Cor 5:10).

Of course, no presentation of the gospel is perfect or includes everything that could be said. Even the best distillation of the gospel requires that the presenter be attentive to the Holy Spirit and to the person and circumstances, adapting it as needed. Often only a part of the message can be shared in a single conversation. Nevertheless, a gospel summary is a useful tool.

3. The Goal of Evangelization

Matthew's version of the great commission makes clear the goal of evangelization: "Go therefore and make disciples of all nations, baptizing them in the name of the Father and of the Son and of the Holy Spirit, teaching them to observe all that I have commanded you" (Mt 28:19–20).

Three elements may be distinguished here. First, it is not sufficient to make converts or church members, but rather *disciples*. According to Matthew, disciples are those whose identity is founded in their relationship with Jesus and who make him the absolute priority of their lives (Mt 8:19–23; 10:37–39; 16:24–26).[90] They share in Jesus' mission, his authority, his self-denial, his persecution, and his reward (Mt 10; 19:29–30).

Second, Jesus commands that disciples be baptized "into" (Greek *eis*) the name of the Father, Son, and Holy Spirit — into a profound relationship with the Persons of the Trinity. The Gospel of John and the letters of Paul explain this relationship and the effects of baptism more fully (Jn 3; Rom 6); Luke depicts these effects in Acts. Throughout the New Testament it is clear that for the apostolic church, the divine life and adoptive sonship received through baptism (and the laying on of hands) was not an abstract doctrine but *a fact of experience* (see especially Acts 8:14–18; 10:44–46; 19:6).[91] Christian initiation was a radically life-transforming event with perceptible outward effects, including an experiential awareness of the Father's love and the lordship of Christ (Rom 5:5; 8:15–16; 1 Cor 12:3b), joy in his salvation (Acts 8:5–8; Rom 15:13; 1 Pet 1:8), overflowing praise (Acts 2:11, 46–47), an eagerness to know the apostles' teaching (Acts 2:42), zeal to boldly proclaim Christ (Acts 4:31; 9:20; 1 Cor 9:16), and service to others through various charisms of the Spirit (1 Cor 12:7–13).

Not surprisingly, today these effects are often missing in those baptized as infants and raised in a secular culture.[92] A closer study of the New Testament data can serve as an impetus for a revitalization of sacramental preparation, especially for Confirmation and the Rite of Christian Initiation for Adults, to inculcate in candidates the dispositions of expectant faith and repentance from sin that will enable the fruits proper to the sacraments to be fully realized.[93] For Catholics already baptized and confirmed, reflection on the New Testament can awaken a new desire to acquire the needed dispositions and appropriate more deeply what they have already received in order to experience the full power of these sacraments.[94]

Finally, Jesus says that his disciples must be taught to observe (or "keep") all that he taught the Twelve. Catechesis about Christian living must follow conversion. Evangelization culminates in a radically new way of life that conforms in every way ("to observe *all*") to the teaching of Christ.

Again it is crucial to preserve the order and distinctiveness of these steps. First comes the proclamation of the *kerygma*, which seeks to elicit a response of faith and repentance, and which issues in baptism for those not already baptized. Catechesis and moral formation *follow* evangelization and conversion (Acts 2:41–42). It is very difficult to adequately catechize those who have not been evangelized and experienced conversion, since they lack the motivation and effective grace of the Spirit to practice what they learn.

4. Paul's Reliance on the Demonstration of the Holy Spirit

Paul is the Church's missionary *par excellence*, and church tradition refers to him as "the Apostle." As such he provides the primary model for bishops, priests, and lay missionaries of subsequent generations insofar as they are called to evangelize.[95]

The primary text in which Paul describes his method of convincing people of the truth of the gospel is 1 Cor 2:4–5. There he writes, "My speech and my proclamation were not with persuasive words of wisdom, but with a demonstration of the Spirit and of power."[96] The context of this remark is Paul's concern that the Corinthian Christians were placing excessive value on ministry that reflected the values of their culture: rhetorical excellence (1 Cor 1:17; 2:1), the "wisdom" of sophisticated philosophical discourse (1:21–25), and social status (1:26–28). This temptation remains today, especially for clergy and scholars educated in philosophy and theology. We, like the Corinthians, are tempted to recoil at simple presentations of the gospel, preferring more sophisticated and respectable engagement with the culture. We are tempted to place our hope in winning the world by the elegant form in which we clothe the truth.

Paul's response to the similar tendency of the Corinthians was that the message of the cross contradicts these priorities entirely. He reminds them that his own preaching that was the origin of their new life in Christ had a completely different basis. Paul preached about the Messiah who "died for our sins … [and] was raised on the third day according to the Scriptures" (1 Cor 15:3–4).

Rather than persuade by words of "wisdom," Paul's proclamation of "Christ crucified" (1:23; 2:1) persuaded by reason of "a demonstration of the Spirit and power." The word translated "demonstration," *apodeixis*, means a "showing forth" or "proof."[97] The two words "Spirit and power" function together to refer to one reality (a figure of speech known as hendiadys), the power of the Holy Spirit. Paul chooses to rely on the proof of the Spirit's power rather than clever philosophical arguments or eloquent oratory for an important reason: "so that your faith might rest not on human wisdom but on the power of God."

A contemporary example may help illustrate Paul's meaning. Some years ago when Peter Williamson was involved in evangelizing university students, he and the group he belonged to tried to articulate the steps in the evangelization process. In addition to such stages as "Arousing Interest," "Presenting the Message," "Answering Objections," and "Inviting a Response," they identified an important step they called "Making it Real," which they recognized was outside their direct power to accomplish. They noticed that in order to believe, people seemed to need to *experience* something that convinced them of the reality of the gospel. Sometimes it was an external event. A Chinese student raised as an atheist was converted when someone prayed over him to be healed of a severe headache. When the pain vanished during the prayer, the student believed and subsequently sought baptism. At other times it was an interior event — for example, an experience of God's love, or a sudden awareness of one's sinfulness and need for forgiveness.

In *Evangelii nuntiandi* (par. 75) Pope Paul VI wrote that "the Holy Spirit is the principal agent of evangelization" and urged that "pastors and theologians — and … the faithful marked by the seal of the Spirit by Baptism — should study more thoroughly the nature and manner of the Holy Spirit's action in evangelization today." St. Paul understood the Spirit to demonstrate the truth of the gospel in at least four ways, which are equally important for effective evangelization today: in the message itself, in the character and demeanor of the evangelist, through signs and wonders, and in the hearts of the listeners.[98]

The Spirit is at work in the message itself

"I am not ashamed of the gospel," Paul declares, "for it is the power of God for salvation to everyone who believes!"[99] As God's message addressed to every person, the gospel is a kind of prophecy. Biblical prophets usually do not supply proofs or satisfy demands for signs (although they sometimes confirm their message by signs at God's initiative). Rather, they speak a message in God's name and, because it is God's word, it bears an anointing, the testimony of God's Spirit. Those who hear must decide at their own risk whether to believe and obey or not.

Paul depicts the gospel as an active agent with a vitality of its own. The word of God is self-diffusing.[100] Paul uses the terms "word of God" and "word of the Lord" almost exclusively to refer to the gospel, the *kerygma*.[101] He tells the Thessalonians that

the "word of the Lord has sounded forth" from them to the sur-
rounding territories (1 Thess 1:8). He asks for prayers that "the
word of the Lord may speed on and triumph (2 Thess 3:1). In 2
Timothy the Apostle Paul, a prisoner bound with chains, con-
trasts his situation to that of the gospel: "but the word of God is
not bound!" (2 Tim 2:8–9).

The vitality of the *kerygma* comes from the Spirit. The word of
God is the "sword of the Spirit" (Eph 6:17). Hebrews 4:12 depicts
God's word as "piercing to the division of soul and of spirit, of
joints and of marrow, and discerning the thoughts and intentions
of the heart."

The powerful self-confirming word of God advances both
through a proclamation of what Jesus did once and for all in the
paschal mystery and through testimony of what Jesus has done
in the life of the proclaimer. One of St. Paul's means of giving
"demonstration of the Spirit's power" was to tell the story of his
encounter with the risen Lord on the road to Damascus (Acts
22 and 26). To this day, one of the most effective ways the Spirit
makes the gospel real to people is through testimony, the evange-
lizer telling how God has acted in his or her life.

The Spirit demonstrates the truth of the message in the character and demeanor of the evangelist

At the beginning of 1 Thessalonians Paul writes, "You know what
kind of men we proved to be among you for your sake" (1 Thess
1:5b). In the next chapter (1 Thess 2:1–12) he reminds the Thessalonians of the love, humility, patience, generosity, hard work,
and total detachment from greed and self-interest that characterized the missionaries who preached to them. The fruit of the
Spirit (Gal 5:22–23) testifies to the truth of the gospel.

How many people have been convinced by the Spirit through
seeing the face of Christ in the *character* of the preacher. We
see dramatic instances of this in the life of Mother Teresa or St.
Francis of Assisi, but the Holy Spirit demonstrates the truth of

the gospel through the character of many ordinary Christians, whether priests, parents, teachers, or friends.[102]

The Spirit of Christ is also manifest and convinces people through the *demeanor* of the evangelist — the courage, conviction, and joy of those who speak his message. The face of the first martyr Stephen, Acts tells us, shone "like the face of an angel" (6:15). To choose a contemporary example, countless millions who watched close-ups of the face of Pope John Paul II were fascinated by what they saw: "Even during the lengthy Masses, his face was not the face of someone presiding over a great public ceremony. It was the face of a man lost in prayer, living in a dimension beyond words."[103]

Acts also recalls the impression made by Peter and John when they stood before the Sanhedrin and proclaimed that "there is no other name under heaven given among men by which we must be saved": "Now when they saw the *boldness* (*parrēsia*) of Peter and John, and perceived that they were uneducated, common men, they were astonished. And they recognized that they had been with Jesus" (Acts 4:12–13).[104]

Thayer's Lexicon defines *parrēsia* as "freedom in speaking," "fearless confidence, cheerful courage." It is the opposite of fear, shame, embarrassment or timidity before powerful political or cultural authorities. Variations of *parrēsia* occur eleven times in Acts to describe the preaching and testimony of the apostles. In Ephesians 6:18–20, Paul asks his readers to pray precisely for this Spirit-inspired boldness: "Pray at all times in the Spirit.... [Pray] also for me, that speech may be given me in opening my mouth *boldly* to proclaim the mystery of the gospel, for which I am an ambassador in chains; that I may declare it *boldly*, as I ought to speak."[105]

Christians today urgently need this grace in view of the scandal of the gospel's claims regarding Christ as the only way of salvation and regarding Scripture's countercultural teaching about marriage and family, sex, and wealth.

The Spirit demonstrates the truth of the message through signs and wonders

A prominent characteristic of Paul's evangelization and that of the early Christians was the presence of "signs and wonders"[106] that confirmed the truth of his message. In Romans 15:18–19 he writes, "For I will not venture to speak of anything except what Christ has accomplished through me to bring the Gentiles to obedience — by word and deed, by the power of signs and wonders, by the power of the Spirit of God." Acts of the Apostles reports some of Paul's signs and wonders and their convincing effects:

- On the island of Cyprus Paul causes temporary blindness to descend on Elymas the magician, because he was opposing the gospel. The proconsul Sergius Paulus is converted (Acts 13:6–12).

- In Philippi, the first European city Paul evangelizes, he casts out a demon from a slave girl. Later, that night an earthquake frees Paul, Silas, and the other prisoners from their chains (Acts 16). The jailer and his household believe and are baptized.

- In Ephesus God does extraordinary miracles by the hands of Paul, "so that handkerchiefs or aprons were carried away from his body to the sick, and diseases left them and the evil spirits came out of them" (Acts 19:11–12). The result? "All the residents of Asia heard the word of the Lord … the name of the Lord Jesus was extolled … and the word of the Lord grew and prevailed mightily" (Acts 19:10, 17, 20).

Paul regards signs and wonders as a credential given by Christ that confirms his apostolic office.[107] He reminds the Corinthians: "The signs of a true apostle were performed among you with utmost patience, with signs and wonders and mighty works" (2 Cor 12:12). It is likely that Paul understood these signs as a continuation of the authority to heal and cast out demons that Jesus gave to his disciples when he sent them to preach the kingdom during his earthly ministry and after the resurrection.[108] The special grace given to presbyters for physical healing attested in James 5:14–16, the biblical foundation of the sacrament of anointing, probably arises from the same apostolic authorization (Mk 6:13).

It is clear, however, that Paul, like the Gospel writers (Mk 16:17–18; Jn 14:12–14) did not regard signs and wonders as confined to apostles. The Holy Spirit gives charisms to those who believe, to each member of the body as the Spirit wills, including gifts of healing and miracles (1 Cor 12:9–10, 29–30). Paul's letters, other NT writings, and extrabiblical texts all testify that healings, exorcisms, and other miracles were part of the normal experience of the early Church.[109]

The Holy Spirit continues to "demonstrate" the truth of the gospel through signs and wonders in our day.

- In June 2012, ZENIT reported on a bishop whose diocese in northeastern India that has grown more than 40% in thirty-five years. He attributes that growth to many supernatural healings his local church is experiencing.[110]

- A priest from the Caribbean who studied in the licentiate (STL) program in the New Evangelization at Sacred Heart Major Seminary reports frequent physical healings following administration of the sacrament of anointing in his hospital ministry. Many priests have similar stories.

- A priest student from India reports about the Divine Retreat Centre run by the Vincentian Congregation in southwest India at Potta-Muringoor. Since 1990 over 10 million people have come to hear preaching and to pray for their needs. Many miracles accompany the proclamation of the gospel and hundreds of thousands have been converted. At the Centre, weeklong retreats are held year-round, and the average number of participants is 15,000 people. (Testimonies of healing and conversion can be read online at www.drcm.org/testimonies.)

- The Spirit uses laypeople as well as priests. Damian Stayne, a layman and member of the *Cor et Lumen Christi* community in England, has witnessed thousands of remarkable healings in his ministry over the last few years. Video recordings of testimonies to miracles are available on the community's website (www .coretlumenchristi.org).

- A few years ago a lay alumna of Sacred Heart Major Seminary visited a friend of hers in the intensive care unit of the hospital. The friend had been in a coma for two weeks, having suffered a massive infection. Because of multiple organ failure, the doctor considered her beyond help. She was scheduled to have the respirator removed in two days. The former student writes, "As I drove to the hospital I kept hearing the words 'Advent is a season of joyful expectation' so when I got to intensive care unit I [laid my hand on her shoulder and] prayed with the full expectation that God would heal her — not 'hope' that God would but 'expectation' that He would. They removed the respirator early on Monday morning and she immediately sat up straight, perfectly alert and lucid and breathing of her own accord. When I visited her a few weeks later she was filled with joy and recovering her strength."[111]

In contemporary culture characterized by what recent popes have called "practical atheism," signs and wonders fulfill an important role in demonstrating the reality of a God who acts in history and desires to be at the center of our lives.

The Spirit confirms the truth of the gospel in the hearts of the listeners

Paul reminds the Christians in Thessalonica how they *experienced* this word when he evangelized them. "For we know, brothers loved by God, that he has chosen you, because our gospel came to you not only in word, but also in power and in the Holy Spirit and with full conviction" (1 Thess 1:4–5). When Paul preached, his listeners experienced not just words, but power, a dynamism that made a deep impression on them. Their experience was like that of the disciples of Emmaus who said, "Were not our hearts burning within us as he spoke to us on the way and opened the Scriptures to us?" (Lk 24:32).

Paul explains, "faith comes from hearing, and hearing comes by the preaching of Christ" (Rom 10:17). When the gospel is proclaimed, the Holy Spirit works in people's hearts, convinces them of the truth, and attracts them to Jesus. The Holy Spirit also convicts people of their sinfulness.[112] When Peter preached on Pentecost morning, the crowd was "cut to the heart and said…. What must we do?" (Acts 2:37).

The sign of the Spirit's presence is a joy that is sometimes otherwise inexplicable, as in the case of the Thessalonians to whom Paul wrote: "you received the word in much affliction, with joy inspired by the Holy Spirit" (1 Thess 1:6).[113]

Faith, prayer, spiritual warfare

If the Church today wishes to rely, like St. Paul, on the power of the Spirit to "make the gospel real" when she evangelizes, the keys are faith, prayer, and awareness of the spiritual combat that evangelization entails.

Like Jesus in the Synoptic Gospels, Paul stresses the primacy of faith (e.g., Gal 3:2–7).[114] Evangelizers must avoid putting their faith in human means — the endorsement of the rich or powerful, skillful use of new media, well-considered documents and programs, astute sociological or theological analysis. While human means are necessary, evangelizers who wish to imitate St. Paul must rather learn to exercise faith and to "pray constantly" (see 1 Thess 5:16–20). The influence of Enlightenment scientism and rationalism and the resulting "practical atheism" of Western culture have weakened the faith of Christians, including that of Church leaders. All who have been raised or educated under this influence must make a conscious effort to discern and reject the habits of unbelief they have acquired. Jesus instructs Thomas: "Do not be unbelieving any more but believe" (Jn 20:27).

Paul directs the members of his churches toward prayer (Rom 12:11; Eph 5:18–20; 1 Thess 5:19; see Lk 11:9–13). Contemporary evangelizers seeking to imitate Paul (1 Cor 4:16; 11:1; Phil 3:17) will seek the guidance of the Spirit for their mission as Paul did (Acts 16:6–10). They will pray that the Spirit anoint the good news about Jesus, embolden their testimony (Acts 4:29–31; Eph 6:18–20), and move the hearts of those to whom they speak (Col 4:2–4; 1 Tim 2:1–4). Finally, they will learn to pray with confidence that God will answer, sometimes even with "signs and wonders" (Mk 11:22–24; 16:17–20). Even when God answers differently than they ask, they can be sure that if they ask the heavenly Father for bread, that he will never give them a stone (Mt 7:7–11).

Just as Jesus' proclamation of the kingdom entailed binding the strong man and taking what he previously held (Mt 12:28–29), Paul also understands Christian life and evangelization as a struggle not merely "against flesh and blood, but against the rulers, against the authorities, against the cosmic powers over this present darkness, against the spiritual forces of evil in the heavenly places" (Eph 6:12). To evangelize means to free people from the power of Satan (Acts 26:18) and to successfully transfer them to Christ's reign (Col 1:13). This requires awareness of the spiritual battle, familiarity with Satan's wiles (2 Cor 11:4), putting on the "whole armor of God" and standing firm (Eph 6:10–11, 13–17), and "prayer at all times in the Spirit" (Eph 6:18–20). Many have observed that it is the devil's ploy either to exaggerate or conceal his activity. It is therefore not surprising that it is politically incorrect and intellectually unacceptable in our world to speak or act as though the devil were real. When, however, Catholics dare to pray, speak, and act with *parrēsia* in light of the worldview taught by Jesus and Paul, they experience the "demonstration of the Spirit" and the advance of the gospel.

5. Paul's Missionary Practice

Besides his reliance on the Spirit, many other aspects of Paul's missionary approach hold promise for the New Evangelization. We will briefly mention a few.

Building Christian communities

Rather than aim at the conversion of individuals, Paul sought to establish communities of believers who could support one another in living a way of life that differed from their pagan neighbors. He recognized that the Holy Spirit dwells in such communities, gifting the members to "edify" or build up one another in their relationship with Christ (1 Cor 12). The role of both itinerant ministers and the community's principal leaders ("apostles, prophets, evangelists, pastors, and teachers") was "to equip the saints for the work of ministry, for building up the body of Christ" (Eph 4:11–12). The central Pauline metaphor and model for ministry in the Church is the human body in which each member has its distinctive ability (*charism*) and function (Rom 12:4–8; 1 Cor 12:12–30). When each part is working properly, the community "makes bodily growth and upbuilds itself in love" (Eph 4:16). Communities like this are self-sustaining.[115]

In recent times some ecclesial movements are providing models for the New Evangelization precisely in their recovery of the communal dimension of Christian life described in Acts and the Pauline letters. Many are also seeking and exercising charisms of the Spirit for building up Christ's body.

Collaboration and teamwork in ministry

Another respect in which Paul's example is instructive for the New Evangelization is in the collaborative way that Paul worked with others in mission. Nearly one hundred names are associated with Paul in the New Testament, thirty-six in fairly close collaboration.[116] Evangelizing and pastoring in teams, rather than as individuals, brings the advantages of spiritual support and protection, communal discernment, diverse charisms, and the testimony of multiple witnesses. Jesus himself established the precedent, sending out his disciples in pairs.

The implications of these biblical examples for the Church today include the importance of priests living and serving together, rather than as isolated individuals, and the collaboration of clergy and lay people in ministry teams.

Ministry formation through discipleship and mentoring

Paul's example is also instructive in regard to the formation of evangelizers and pastoral ministers. Paul's many coworkers learned by living with him, by observing his way of life, and by watching him preach, teach and evangelize (Acts 20:18–21, 31–35 et passim; 2 Tim 3:10–11). From there they progressed to fulfilling ministry assignments from Paul and some eventually to governing churches on their own. This method both inculcates character traits through personal relationship and example[117] and effective ministry skills through observation and hands-on experience.

This New Testament paradigm for leadership formation is manifest in Jesus' training of the Twelve and implicit in his command, "Go and make disciples…." Analogously, Paul counsels Timothy, "what you heard from me through many witnesses entrust to faithful people who will have the ability to teach others as well" (2 Tim 2:2).

Today the formation of pastoral ministers in the Catholic Church diverges greatly from the pattern followed by Jesus and by Paul. Contemporary formation of clergy and other pastoral ministers is largely academic and institutional, offering relatively little opportunity for practice in evangelization and pastoral skills or of learning directly from exemplary pastors and evangelizers. The community life of some institutes and ecclesial movements offer models of how such formation might be carried out today that could be adopted for the formation of diocesan clergy and lay leaders. The New Evangelization calls for a creative rethinking of how the Church forms pastoral ministers at all levels. To the degree that it is possible, mentoring and hands-on training in evangelization and pastoral care under the supervision of an experienced, gifted leader should be maximized.

The Role of Scripture in Church life and ministry formation

Finally, Paul's emphasis on Scripture in the ministry and formation of evangelizers and pastoral ministers is noteworthy. The many allusions to the Old Testament Scriptures found in the New Testament suggest that communal reading and explanation of Scripture was far more characteristic of the life of the early Church that it is of the Church today.[118]

Explicit indications, especially in the Pastoral Letters, show that this was a deliberate pastoral practice. Paul tells Timothy, "Till I come, attend to the public reading of Scripture, to preaching, to teaching" (1 Tim 4:13). Paul exhorts Timothy, and by extension, all pastoral ministers, about honing their skills in communicating God's word: "Do your best to present yourself to God as one approved, a worker who has no need to be ashamed, rightly handling the word of truth" (2 Tim 2:15; cf. 1 Tim 4:16).

Finally, in the text that we think of in relation to the *inspiration* of Scripture, Paul emphasizes rather the *usefulness* of Scripture and its virtual sufficiency for ministry formation:

> All Scripture is inspired by God and *useful* for teaching, for reproof, for correction, and for training in righteousness, *so that* the man of God may be competent, fully equipped for every good work. (2 Tim 3:16–17)

As the inspired word of God, Scripture is efficacious (Isa 55:10–11). *Verbum Domini* speaks of the sacramentality of the word: it effects what it signifies.[119] Above all this is true in evangelization, since "faith comes from hearing and hearing through the word of Christ" (Rom 10:17).

In *Verbum Domini* the Holy Father echoes *Dei Verbum* 25 in recommending frequent Bible reading and the familiarity with Scripture that it engenders to bishops (79), priests (80), deacons (81), consecrated persons (83), laypeople (84), and families (85). In at least eight places *Verbum Domini* speaks of the importance of being "familiar with the word of God."[120]

Despite the emphasis on reading and studying Scripture in *Dei Verbum* and magisterial documents up to the present, this kind of familiarity with the word of God remains an elusive goal. Among seminarians preparing for priesthood — those for whom the standards are highest — familiarity with Scripture remains disturbingly low.[121] Scripture formation in undergraduate seminary formation is negligible, and graduate theology requirements in most U.S. seminaries do not include biblical languages and often fail to cover significant parts of the biblical canon.

Conclusion

As the Church considers how to promote a new evangelization, we would do well to recall and build upon the 2008 Synod on the Word of God in the Life and Mission of the Church, summed up in *Verbum Domini*. More importantly, bishops, priests, and all who exercise leadership in the Church would benefit from studying what Scripture itself says about the task, message, and goal of evangelization and reflect upon the perennial paradigm of evangelization set forth in the New Testament and in the life and writings of the Apostle to the Gentiles.

About the Authors

of

Biblical Orientations for the
New Evangelization

Mary Healy is associate professor of Sacred Scripture at Sacred Heart Major Seminary in Detroit. She is the author of *Men and Women Are from Eden* (Cincinnati: Servant, 2005) and coeditor of three books on biblical interpretation. She is also coeditor of the Catholic Commentary on Sacred Scripture and author of its first volume, *The Gospel of Mark* (Grand Rapids: Baker, 2008).

Peter Williamson holds the Adam Cardinal Maida Chair in Sacred Scripture at Sacred Heart Major Seminary. He is the author of *Catholic Principles for Interpreting Scripture* (Rome: Biblical Institute, 2001) and coeditor with Ralph Martin of *John Paul II and the New Evangelization* (St. Anthony Messenger, 2006). He is also coeditor of the Catholic Commentary on Sacred Scripture and author of its volume on *Ephesians* (Grand Rapids: Baker, 2009).

Endnotes

Chapter I

1   It is beyond the scope of this book to elaborate on how one can grow in holiness, but I have published a book that lays out the stages of the whole spiritual journey that many find helpful. *The Fulfillment of All Desire: A Guidebook for the Journey to God Based on the Wisdom of the Saints*. It is available in several formats, and a Study Guide and DVD version are also available. All are available on our website at: www .renewalministries.net (click on "Store").

2   Pope John Paul II, "The Task of the Latin American Bishop," *Origins* 12 (March 24, 1983): 659-62.

3   Pope John Paul II, "Address to Bishops of Latin America," *L'Osservatore Romano*, English Language Edition, October 21, 1992.

4   In chapter IV we will consider in some detail the necessary role of the Holy Spirit in activating the New Evangelization.

5   For example, in another diocese while the Catholic population of the ten counties of the diocese declined by 3.25%, the drop in Mass attendance was five times greater — a 16.37% decline since the year 2000. There has been an even more precipitous decline in that period in baptisms (-32.81%), in marriages (-44.38%), and in RCIA participation (-57.7%). The diocese notes that the reported decline is not confined to one area of the diocese or clustered in a small number of urban parishes but is widespread.

6   The Center for Applied Research in the Apostolate (CARA) provides exhaustive statistics, continually updated, on many Catholic metrics. Their home page (www.cara.georgetown.edu) contains a section titled "Church Statistics" that opens to this information.

7   See Jim Graves, "Where Are the Priests?" in *National Catholic Register*, July 17–30, 2011, p. 1, ff. While Hispanics now comprise nearly 40% of the total U.S. Catholic population (and over 50% of the Catholic youth population), only 10-15% of the priests ordained each year are Hispanic. Only 9% of the bishops are Hispanic. In heavily Hispanic dioceses like Los Angeles and Phoenix ordinations of any kind are shockingly rare. In Los Angeles, the largest archdiocese in the U.S., only three

men were ordained in 2010, and only six in 2011. In Phoenix only three were ordained in 2010 and none in 2011.

8   While there has been growth in the West, Southwest, and South, a growth that is largely due to Hispanic immigration, not growth through evangelization, the statistics about the outflow from the Catholic Church in second- and third-generation Hispanic Catholic immigrants are not encouraging. See Edwin Hernández, with Rebecca Burwell and Jeffrey Smith, "A Study of Hispanic Catholics: Why Are They Leaving the Catholic Church? Implications for the New Evangelization," in *The New Evangelization: Overcoming the Obstacles,* ed. Steven Boguslawski and Ralph Martin (New York: Paulist Press, 2008), 109-141.

9   For a recent comprehensive study of the religious beliefs of American youth, see Christian Smith with Melinda Lundquist Denton, *Soul Searching: The Religious and Spiritual Lives of American Teenagers* (New York: Oxford University Press, 2005), 166.

10   John Lamont, "What Was Wrong with Vatican II," *New Black-friars,* v. 99, no. 1013, Jan 2007, 92-93. See also John Lamont, "Why the Second Vatican Council Was a Good Thing and Is More Important Than Ever," *New Oxford Review* (July/August, 2005): 32-36, in which he identifies the positive aspects of Vatican II.

11   Ratzinger, *The Yes of Jesus Christ* (New York: The Crossroad Publishing Company, 2005), 35.

12   Timothy E. Byerley, *The Great Commission: Models of Evangelization in American Catholicism* (New York: Paulist Press, 2008), ix.

13   Drawn from a book by Nancy T. Ammerman, *Pillars of Faith* (Berkeley: University of California Press, 2005) 117, 134.

14   Avery Dulles, "John Paul II and the New Evangelization" in Avery Dulles, *Church and Society* (New York: Fordham University Press, 2008), 96-100.

Chapter II

15   I did my doctoral dissertation on the topic being discussed in this chapter. It has now been published in book form under the title: *Will Many Be Saved? What Vatican II Actually Teaches and Its Implications for the New Evangelization.* Available on our website, www .renewalministries.net (click on "Store").

Chapter III

16   Deacon James Keating has published several articles that touch on the relationship between clergy and laity. "Priestly Spirituality, Seminary Formation, and Lay Mission" in *Seminary Journal*, Fall 2007; "How Can Catholic Spirituality Be More at the Heart of Priestly Formation," *Seminary Journal*, Winter 2005; and "Sharing in the Pastoral Charity of Christ: Priestly Formation as Spirituality," *Seminary Journal,* Winter 2008.

17   I am happy to report that the seminary where I teach, Sacred Heart Major Seminary, in the Archdiocese of Detroit, has implemented a new focus in our seminary teaching and training, summed up in our new motto: "Preparing Heralds for the New Evangelization." With more than 100 seminarians and 350 lay students in various degree and certificate programs we are grateful for what the Lord is doing. www.shms.edu

18   A book that is sensitive to the actual situation of Catholic parishes today and the challenge of moving from "maintenance to mission" is *From Maintenance to Mission,* Fr. Robert Rivers (New York: Paulist Press, 2005). Also, the book edited by myself and Peter Williamson, *John Paul II and the New Evangelization* (Cincinnati: Servant/St. Anthony, 2006), contains many chapters that demonstrate an unfolding of the "new evangelization" in a variety of parish settings and mission contexts. Sherry Weddell's book *Forming Intentional Disciples* (Huntington, IN: Our Sunday Visitor, 2012) gives a sobering evaluation of where Catholics are at today as regards discipleship and lays out detailed wisdom to improve the situation. Fr. Michael White and Tom Corcoran have produced a book, *Rebuilt: Awakening the Faithful, Reaching the Lost, Making Church Matter* (Notre Dame, IN: Ave Maria Press, 2013), that gives a penetrating diagnosis of why parishes are dying and challenging advice for turning them around.

19   See for example Archbishop Robert Carlson's Pastoral Letter on Evangelization: *Go and Announce the Gospel of the Lord*, archstl.org/files/Pastoral_Letter.pdf (accessed April 15, 2013).

20   I've coedited two collections of essays on the New Evangelization that elaborate on many of the issues being treated in this book. The first is Ed. Ralph Martin and Peter Williamson, *John Paul II and the New Evangelization: How You Can Bring the Good News to Others*; and the second, Ed. Steven Boguslawski and Ralph Martin, *The New Evangelization: Overcoming the Obstacles*. Both are available on our website: www.renewalministries.net (click on "Store").

Chapter IV

21   Edward D. O'Connor, C.S.C., *The Pentecostal Movement in the Catholic Church* (Notre Dame: Ave Maria Press, 1971), cites several instances in which Pope John XXIII links the meaning of Vatican II to a "new Pentecost" (287-289).

22   When the papal document being quoted is clearly mentioned in the text the number in parenthesis at the end of the quotation is the section number from the document.

23   Pope Paul VI, Apostolic Exhortations *Evangelii nuntiandi* ("Evangelization in the Modern World"), December 8, 1975, and *Gaudete in Domino* ("On Christian Joy"), May 9, 1975.

24   Pope Paul VI, General Audience, November 29, 1972.

25   *L'Osservatore Romano*, English Language Edition, June 3, 1998; "This is the day the Lord has made! Holy Father holds historic meeting with ecclesial movements and new communities"; 1-2. Also available as an appendix in a document published by Pontificium Consilium Pro Laicis as part of their *Laity Today Series*: "Movements in the Church: Proceedings of the World Congress of the Ecclesial Movements," Rome, May 27–29, 1998," Vatican City 1999.

26   NMI 40.

27   NMI 58.

28   Homily given by Pope Benedict XVI on June 3, 2006, published in *New Outpourings of the Spirit*, 132- 133.

29   Pope Benedict XVI, General Audience of September 28, 2005. "I hope that the Holy Spirit will be ever more welcome in the hearts of believers and that the 'culture of Pentecost,' which is so necessary in our day, might continue to spread."

30   Pope Benedict XVI, *Homily on the Feast of the Baptism of the Lord*, January 13, 2008.

31   Pope Benedict XVI, *Angelus Address*, January 13, 2008.

32   Pope Benedict XVI, 23rd World Youth Day, Sydney, Australia, July 23, 2008.

33   Pope Benedict XVI, "Let Baptism of the Holy Spirit purify every heart," given May 11, 2008, printed in *L'Osservatore Romano*, English Edition, May 14, 2008, No. 20, p. 1.

34   Pope Benedict XVI, Homily Given at Washington Nationals Stadium, April 17, 2008. www.vatican.va/holy_father/benedict_xvi/

homilies/2008/documents/hf_ben-xvi_hom_20080417_washington-stadium_en.html (accessed April 3, 2013).

35   Pope Benedict XVI, Homily at St. Patrick's Cathedral, April 19, 2008.

36   Fr. Francis Sullivan, "Baptism in the Holy Spirit": A Catholic Interpretation of the Pentecostal Experience," *Gregorianum* 55/1 (1974), 49-68. Many of the books cited below contain both testimonies of the effects of being baptized in the Spirit by those who have experienced such, as well as theological summaries of the effects. The testimonies and the theological summaries are remarkably similar. It is worth noting that many of the theologians writing on the issue of baptism of the Spirit, such as Fr. Raniero Cantalamessa and Cardinal Suenens, were living devout and very dedicated Catholic lives and yet still testify to a significant "turning point" when they prayed for a renewal of their baptism in the Spirit, understood as the graces of Christian initiation.

37   Paul Josef Cordes, *Call to Holiness: Reflections on the Catholic Charismatic Renewal* (Collegeville: The Liturgical Press, 1997), 11-13.

38   Léon Joseph Cardinal Suenens, *A New Pentecost?* (New York: The Seabury Press, 1975), 212-227.

39   Raniero Cantalamessa, O.F.M. Cap., trans. Marsha Daigle-Williamson, *Sober Intoxication of the Spirit: Filled with the Fullness of God* (Cincinnati: Servant Books, 2003), 158-161.

40   "If we were to be more precise we would not talk of receiving the Baptism in the Holy Spirit, but of renewing the Baptism in the Spirit." Kevin and Dorothy Ranaghan, *Catholic Pentecostals* (New York: Paulist, 1969), 151.

41   Pope Benedict XVI, "Let Baptism of the Holy Spirit purify every heart," Given May 11, 2008, *L'Osservatore Romano*, English Edition, May 14, 2008, p. 1.

42   Raniero Cantalamessa, O.F.M. Cap., trans. Marsha Daigle-Williamson, *Sober Intoxication of the Spirit: Filled with the Fullness of God* (Cincinnati: St. Anthony Messenger Press, 2005), 1-20.

43   Kilian McDonnell and George T. Montague, *Christian Initiation and Baptism in the Spirit: Evidence from the First Eight Centuries*, 2nd ed. (Collegeville, MN: Liturgical Press, 1994), 339.

44   I've recently participated in the development of a high-quality DVD series of talks modeled on the popular Life in the Spirit Seminars that are intended for personal or group use in helping people experience more of the Holy Spirit in their lives. The DVD is called *As By A*

New Pentecost and is available on our website, www.renewalministries
.net (click on "Store"). Another valuable resource has been developed
by Christlife (www.christlife.org), who has also developed three very
useful DVD series helping people to "Discover Christ, Follow Christ,
and Share Christ," available on their website. The first series has been
put into book form titled *Discover Christ: Developing a Personal Relationship with Jesus,* coauthored by Bert Ghezzi and David Nodar and
published by OSV.

Chapter V

45   Francis Martin, "The Spirit of the Lord is Upon Me: The Role of
the Holy Spirit in the Work of Evangelization," in *The New Evangelization: Overcoming the Obstacles,* ed. Boguslawski & Martin, 72-73. See
also 74-76.

46   St. Faustina Kowalska, *Diary: Divine Mercy in My Soul,* Third
edition with revisions (Stockbridge, MA: Association of Marian Help-
ers, 1996), #965, pp. 374-375.

47   Ibid., #741, pp. 296-297.

48   Ibid., #741, p. 297.

49   Catherine of Siena, *The Dialogue,* trans. Suzanne Noffke, O.P.,
The Classics of Western Spirituality (New York/Mahwah: Paulist Press,
1980), chapter 38, pp. 80-81; chapter 42, pp. 86-87.

50   Catherine of Siena, *The Dialogue,* chapter 41, p. 83.

51   Bernard of Clairvaux, *On the Song of Songs,* Volume IV, trans.
Irene Edmonds (Kalamazoo, MI: Cistercian Publications, 1980), Sermon 72, nos. 9-10, pp. 72-73.

52   Catherine of Siena, *The Dialogue,* chapter 41, p. 83.

53   Ibid., chapter 41, pp. 83-84.

54   Ibid., chapter 43, pp. 88-89.

55   Ibid., chapter 43, p. 89.

56   Bernard of Clairvaux, *On the Song of Songs,* Volume III, trans.
Kilian Walsh, O.C.S.O., and Irene Edmonds (Kalamazoo, MI: Cistercian
Publications, 1979), Sermon 87, no. 1, p. 97.

57   Catherine of Siena, *The Dialogue,* chapter 41, p. 85.

58   Bernard of Clairvaux, *On the Song of Songs,* Volume I, trans.
Kilian Walsh, O.C.S.O. (Kalamazoo, MI: Cistercian Publications, 1971),
Sermon 20, no. 2, p. 148.

Chapter VI

59   My colleagues and I will continue to comment on these issues in our free monthly newsletter, which can be obtained by going to our website, www.renewalministries.net, and clicking on "Newsletter."

Appendix

60   The New Evangelization was first articulated by Pope John Paul II as a summons for the Church in an address to Latin American bishops in Port-au-Prince, Haiti, on May 9, 1983 (*Origins* 12 [March 24, 1983], 659-62), although he had used the term "new evangelization" in an earlier homily in Mogila, Poland (June 9, 1979). He subsequently repeated the call numerous times, particularly in his encyclical *Redemptoris missio* (1990), 3, and his apostolic letter *Novo millennio ineunte* (2001), 40.

61   *Verbum Domini*, 73.

62   *Dei Verbum*, 21; emphasis added.

63   *Verbum Domini*, 17.

64   See especially 13, 61.

65   Cf. CCC 85-86. The Pontifical Biblical Commission, in its *Instruction on Scripture and Christology* (1984), distinguishes between the "auxiliary" language of ordinary Church discourse and the "referential" language of the Scriptures (1.2.2.1).

66   See Raniero Cantalamessa, *Lenten Sermon to Benedict XVI and the Roman Curia* (Feb. 29, 2008), 4.

67   *Evangelii nuntiandi*, 51.

68   For example, Paul presupposes acceptance of the Torah and Prophets when addressing Jewish audiences in Pisidian Antioch and Thessalonica (Acts 13, 17), whereas he begins with the doctrine of God when addressing Gentile audiences in Lystra and Athens (Acts 14, 17).

69   We hope that other scholars will take this study further and serve the New Evangelization by considering in more detail these and other aspects of evangelization in the New Testament. A systematic study of evangelization in the Synoptics, the Gospel of John, Acts, and Paul's letters in view of contemporary culture and the New Evangelization could be of great value.

70   In a biblical context, Jesus' command to wait for the Spirit sets the stage for a transmission of his prophetic Spirit to his successors, just

as Moses' spirit was transmitted to Joshua (Deut 34:9) and Elijah's to Elisha (2 Kings 2:9). See Luke Timothy Johnson, *The Acts of the Apostles*, Sacra Pagina (Collegeville, MN: Liturgical 1992), 30-31.

71   Whereas Paul in his letters reflects theologically on the gift of the Spirit and its interior effects, Luke *shows* these effects through the visible activity of the church. For Paul, to be filled with the Holy Spirit is to be filled with the love of God (cf. Rom 5:5) and an interior revelation of Christ (cf. 1 Cor 2:9-12). For Luke, both these effects are manifest in the dramatic transformation that takes place in the apostles following Pentecost. For theological studies of the Spirit's work as presented in Acts see George Montague, *The Holy Spirit: Growth of a Biblical Tradition* (New York: Paulist, 1976), 134-36, 205-206; and Craig Keener, *The Spirit in the Gospels and Acts: Divine Purity and Power* (Peabody, MA: Hendrickson, 1997), 190-213. For an examination of the Spirit's revelatory work in Paul, see Mary Healy, "Knowledge of the Mystery: A Study of Pauline Epistemology," in Mary Healy and Robin Parry (eds.), *The Bible and Epistemology: Biblical Soundings on the Knowledge of God* (Milton Keynes, UK: Paternoster, 2007), 134-58.

72   Divine power (*dynamis*) is a distinguishing feature of the Christian mission throughout Acts (3:12; 4:7, 33; 6:8; 8:19; 19:11), as it was of Jesus' ministry (Lk 4:14; Acts 10:38).

73   Pope Paul VI, *Evangelii nuntiandi*, 75.

74   See, for example, Pope John Paul II, Address to New Communities and Lay Movements, May 30, 1998; Joseph Cardinal Ratzinger, *The Ratzinger Report* (San Francisco: Ignatius, 1985), 43-44.

75   Cf. especially Lk 5:29-30; 7:34; 19:5.

76   "Why have so many left the Church? While this is an important question, the more important question is, "Why are we sitting around tending the ninety-nine and not going after the one who has been lost (Mt 18:12-14)?"… One sheep wanders away, then another, then another! Soon we are forced to ask why we are tending the fifty sheep and not going after the other fifty who have been lost" (Bishop Earl Boyea, Pastoral Letter "Go and Announce the Gospel of the Lord," April 5, 2012, p. 20).

77   See Robert S. Rivers, *From Maintenance to Mission. Evangelization and the Revitalization of the Parish* (New York: Paulist, 2005).

78   Cantalamessa, Advent homily, Dec. 2, 2005, available at www .zenit.org/article-14735?l=english (accessed Nov. 27, 2012).

79   This theme is ubiquitous in the New Testament: Mt 11:20-24; 12:41-42; Jn 3:18, 36; 12:48; Acts 13:46; Rom 2:7-8; 11:14; 1 Cor 9:22; 2 Thess 2:12; 1 Tim 1:16; Heb 2:3; 12:25; 1 Jn 5:12. Cf. CCC 161, 678-79.

This paragraph and the next are indebted to Ralph Martin, *Will Many Be Saved?* (Grand Rapids: Eerdmans, 2012).

80   See ibid., especially 195-208.

81   *Instrumentum*, 85.

82   Cf. Acts 5:42; 8:4, 12, 35; 1 Cor 1:17; Gal 1:16; Eph 3:8. The term *kerygma* (the "message," or essential content of the gospel) appears in Rom 16:25; 1 Cor 1:21; 2:4, 15:14; 2 Tim 4:17; Titus 1:3.

83   *Evangelii nuntiandi*, 27; cf. *Redemptoris missio*, 44.

84   "The New Evangelization and Preaching the *Kerygma*," *Bulletin Dei Verbum*, English Edition, 2012, no. 2-3, p. 24.

85   Ibid.

86   Pope John Paul II, *Catechesi tradendae*, 19.

87   Cesclas Spicq notes that in both secular and biblical Greek *euangelizomai* and its cognate nouns express the gratuitousness of the gifts announced and the resulting joy (*Theological Lexicon of the New Testament*, trans. James Ernest [Peabody, MA: Hendrickson, 1994], vol. 2, 86-87).

88   C. H. Dodd provides a classic analysis of these sermons in *The Apostolic Preaching and Its Developments* (Grand Rapids: Baker, 1980).

89   These five points are present in an elegantly condensed form in paragraph 1 of the *Catechism*. The first four are also loosely similar to a popular Protestant evangelistic tool known as the "Four Spiritual Laws." Finally, these points follow the movement of the biblical story of salvation considered as narrative: exposition, conflict, climax, resolution, denouement.

90   The Catherine of Siena Institute, a program dedicated to equipping parishes for the formation of lay Catholics for evangelization, has adopted the term "intentional disciples" to emphasize the profound choice and commitment entailed in discipleship. See Sherry Weddell, *Forming Intentional Disciples: The Path to Knowing and Following Jesus* (Huntington, IN: Our Sunday Visitor, 2012).

91   That was the case in both the New Testament, and the patristic era is demonstrated by Kilian McDonnell and George T. Montague, *Christian Initiation and Baptism in the Spirit: Evidence from the First Eight Centuries*, 2nd ed. (Collegeville, MN: Liturgical Press, 1994).

92   For those baptized as infants and raised in an environment of vibrant faith (an increasingly rare situation today), a more organic and continuous growth toward full personal acceptance of the faith is possible.

93   The dispositions necessary for Baptism and Confirmation to bear fruit include a lively understanding of the gospel and the gifts God intends for his people, personal faith in Jesus, repentance, and the desire to do God's will. If someone who received the sacraments as an infant grows up in a vibrant community of faith, the effects of the sacraments unfold naturally as these dispositions develop. However, grace remains bound or dormant in Catholics to the degree that they do not acquire these dispositions. See Raniero Cantalamessa, *Sober Intoxication of the Spirit*, 41-43. In the part of his *Summa Theologica* devoted to Baptism (III, Q. 66-71), Thomas Aquinas indicates the importance of adequate preparation and the proper dispositions for the efficacy of Baptism, including repentance and faith, devotion, sincerity, instruction, exorcism, and responsible and knowledgeable godparents. See also Augustine, *Sermon*, 269.2.

94   Various programs are available that have proven effective at helping people do so, such as Cursillo, Alpha, the Life in the Spirit Seminar, Discovering Christ, the Philip course, and Ignatian retreats.

95   When speaking of Paul we refer to the canonical Paul, that is, the picture of Paul and his mission that emerges from considering Acts and all the letters that bear Paul's name. This part of our presentation is adapted from Peter Williamson's article "Effective Proclamation: Demonstration of the Spirit and Power" in *Soter* 34:62 (2010) available at www.vddb.laba .lt/fedora/get/LT-eLABa-0001:J.04~2010~ISSN_1392-7450.N_34_62 .PG_71-79/DS.002.1.01.ARTIC (accessed Aug. 8, 2012).

96   Our interpretation of this and the related texts mentioned primarily follows Gordon D. Fee, *God's Empowering Presence* (Peabody, MA: Hendrickson, 1994). I also draw on David E. Garland, *First Corinthians* (Grand Rapids, Baker Academic, 2003), J.D.G. Dunn, *The Theology of Paul the Apostle* (Grand Rapids: Eerdmans, 1998), and George Montague, *The Holy Spirit: The Growth of a Biblical Tradition* (Eugene, OR: Wipf and Stock, 2006).

97   For a good overview of the role of *apodeixis* in the context of Greco-Roman rhetoric, see E. J. Schnabel, *Paul the Missionary* (Downers Grove, IL: InterVarsity, 2008), 344-47.

98   For an overview of the role of the Spirit in the proclamation and hearing of the gospel and in conversion, see Gordon Fee, *God's Empowering Presence*, 846-64.

99   Rom 1:16. See the treatment of Paul's understanding of the self-diffusing nature of the word in Robert L. Plummer, *Paul's Understanding of the Church's Mission* (Colorado Springs: Paternoster, 2006), 50-64.

100   Plummer, *Paul's Understanding*, 61-67, 141-42.

101   For the distinction between *kerygma* and *didache* and perspectives on recovering the *kerygma*, see Raniero Cantalamessa, *Remember Jesus Christ* (Ijamsville, MD: The Word Among Us, 2007), 16-25. For the various ways "word of God" is used in Scripture, see Carlo Martini, *La Parola di Dio alle origini della Chiesa* (Rome: 1980), 56-58.

102   See *Lineamenta*, 22, on the role of witnesses.

103   George Weigel, *Witness to Hope* (New York: HarperCollins, 1999), 364.

104   Immediately after this event the Jerusalem church prays for more of the same grace of the Spirit; see Acts 4:29-31.

105   To give another Pauline example, when Paul tells the Christians in Philippi that their boldness, unity, and freedom from fear — gifts of the Spirit — are a *proof (endeixis)* to their persecutors of impending destruction and of the ultimate salvation of believers (Phil 1:14, 27-28; 2:1-2).

106   "Signs and wonders," a biblical phrase that originally described the miracles God worked through Moses to deliver his people from Egypt, also describes the miracles God works to confirm the preaching of the gospel (Deut 6:2, 26:28; Mk 16:17-20; Acts 4:30; 5:3; 14:3; 15:12; Heb 2:4).

107   It is nevertheless worth noting that in Acts, as in the Gospels, signs and wonders are never performed on demand. Rather, as in the ministry of Jesus, the miracles done by Paul and the other apostles are always in response to needs or requests, or spontaneously, at the initiative of the Spirit.

108   Mt 28:18-20; Mk 16:15-20; Lk 24:45-49; Acts 1:8.

109   One example suffices to show that Paul presupposes signs and wonders as the normal experience in the Church. In Galatians Paul argues for the superiority of faith over works of the law on the basis of his readers' experience: "Let me ask you only this: Did you receive the Spirit by works of the law, or by hearing with faith? Are you so foolish? Having begun with the Spirit, are you now ending with the flesh? Did

you experience so many things in vain?… Does he who supplies the Spirit to you and works miracles among you do so by works of the law, or by hearing with faith?" (Gal 3:2-5).

110   See "Indian Bishop Wonders If Miracles Are Happening" in ZENIT, June 22, 2012.

111   Email message from Mrs. Carol Kean, March 18, 2009.

112   Paul reports this happening in the meetings of the early church: "But if all prophesy, and an unbeliever or outsider enters, he is convicted by all, he is called to account by all, the secrets of his heart are disclosed; and so, falling on his face, he will worship God and declare that God is really among you" (1 Cor 14:24-25).

Sometimes the Holy Spirit is at work, but the person refuses to respond. Acts 24:25 reports that as Paul spoke to the Roman governor Felix "about justice and self-control and future judgment, Felix was alarmed and said, 'Go away for the present; when I have an opportunity I will summon you.'"

113   Likewise 1 Pet 1:8-9 "Although you have not seen him you love him; even though you do not see him now yet believe in him, you rejoice with an indescribable and glorious joy, as you attain the goal of (your) faith, the salvation of your souls."

114   The first three paragraphs of the preface of the *Instrumentum Laboris* provide examples from the Gospels of this type of faith. For more on expectant faith and prayer, see the unpublished paper by Peter S. Williamson, "Doing the Works of Jesus and Greater Works: A Theological Interpretation of John 14:12-14" (available online).

115   See Michael J. Gorman, *Apostle of the Crucified Lord* (Grand Rapids: Eerdmans, 2004), 124-127.

116   See E.E. Ellis, "Coworkers, Paul and His" in Gerald F. Hawthorne, et al., eds., *Dictionary of Paul and His Letters* (Downers Grove, IL: InterVarsity, 1993)183-88.

117   See *Lineamenta*, 22.

118   In the middle of the second century, Justin Martyr describes the liturgy: "the memoirs of the apostles or the writings of the prophets are read for as long as time permits" (*Apology*, 67). If the liturgy today only allows very brief readings and explanation, other fora need to be found for this vital function.

119   Raniero Cantalamessa, the preacher to the papal court, explains that the Greek word translated "inspired" in 2 Tim 3:16, *theo-*

pneustos, has, in addition to this passive sense, an active meaning. Having inspired the words of Scripture, "the Holy Spirit is, as it were, contained in it, lives in it, and enlivens it unceasingly with his own divine breath…. Once and for all time, the Holy Spirit inspired Scripture and now, each time we open the book, Scripture breathes the Holy Spirit!" See Raniero Cantalamessa, *The Mystery of God's Word* (Collegeville, MN: Liturgical, 1994), 80.

120   He begins by speaking of Mary's "familiarity with the word of God" (28), recommending the same for the faithful (62, 64, 84) and for clergy (80). He exhorts "all the People of God, pastors, consecrated persons and the laity, to become increasingly familiar with the sacred Scriptures" (121), and concludes his apostolic exhortation by "remind[ing] all Christians that our personal and communal relationship with God depends on our growing familiarity with the word of God" (124).

121   Biblical *lectio divina* ought not be limited to the Lectionary or to the Office of Readings, which despite their immense value, do not inculcate familiarity with the biblical books themselves. Peter Williamson learned this a few years ago when he gave his Pauline Literature class an anonymous pretest to ascertain their familiarity with Paul's letters. The test listed sixteen well-known Pauline quotations or topics and the titles of the letters attributed to Paul, asking the students to indicate in which letter or letters the topic or quote is found. He then had the students exchange tests and grade them, taking a very generous view of what constituted a correct answer. Out of 16 possible points, the students averaged less than 4. When the highest scores were excluded, the averages drop nearly a point for each group; the most common score was 1 out of 16! What was most surprising was how poorly the seminarians did. These were bright, highly-motivated second-year theologians who had completed their college seminary and pre-theology, attended Mass and prayed the Office daily for a minimum of three years, yet were not familiar with Paul's letters at all.

Notes

Notes

Notes